ZIML Math Competition Book

Division M 2018-2019

Areteem Institute

ZIML Math Competition Book Division M 2018-2019

Edited by   John Lensmire
　　　　　　David Reynoso
　　　　　　Kevin Wang
　　　　　　Kelly Ren

Copyright © 2019 ARETEEM INSTITUTE
WWW.ARETEEM.ORG

PUBLISHED BY ARETEEM PRESS
ALL RIGHTS RESERVED. No part of this publication may be reproduced, stored in a retrieval system, or transmitted, in any form or by any means, electronic, mechanical, photocopying, recording, or otherwise, without prior written permission of the publisher, except for "fair use" or other noncommercial uses as defined in Sections 107 and 108 of the U.S. Copyright Act.

ISBN-10: 1-944863-45-1
ISBN-13: 978-1-944863-45-6

First printing, August 2019.

TITLES PUBLISHED BY ARETEEM PRESS

Cracking the High School Math Competitions (and Solutions Manual) - Covering AMC 10 & 12, ARML, and ZIML
Mathematical Wisdom in Everyday Life (and Solutions Manual) - From Common Core to Math Competitions
Geometry Problem Solving for Middle School (and Solutions Manual) - From Common Core to Math Competitions
Fun Math Problem Solving For Elementary School (and Solutions Manual)

ZIML MATH COMPETITION BOOK SERIES

ZIML Math Competition Book Division E 2016-2017
ZIML Math Competition Book Division M 2016-2017
ZIML Math Competition Book Division H 2016-2017
ZIML Math Competition Book Jr Varsity 2016-2017
ZIML Math Competition Book Varsity Division 2016-2017
ZIML Math Competition Book Division E 2017-2018
ZIML Math Competition Book Division M 2017-2018
ZIML Math Competition Book Division H 2017-2018
ZIML Math Competition Book Jr Varsity 2017-2018
ZIML Math Competition Book Varsity Division 2017-2018
ZIML Math Competition Book Division E 2018-2019
ZIML Math Competition Book Division M 2018-2019
ZIML Math Competition Book Division H 2018-2019
ZIML Math Competition Book Jr Varsity 2018-2019
ZIML Math Competition Book Varsity Division 2018-2019

MATH CHALLENGE CURRICULUM TEXTBOOKS SERIES

Math Challenge I-A Pre-Algebra and Word Problems
Math Challenge I-B Pre-Algebra and Word Problems
Math Challenge I-C Algebra
Math Challenge II-A Algebra
Math Challenge II-B Algebra
Math Challenge III Algebra

Math Challenge I-A Geometry
Math Challenge I-B Geometry
Math Challenge I-C Topics in Algebra
Math Challenge II-A Geometry
Math Challenge II-B Geometry
Math Challenge III Geometry
Math Challenge I-A Counting and Probability
Math Challenge I-B Counting and Probability
Math Challenge I-C Geometry
Math Challenge II-A Combinatorics
Math Challenge II-B Combinatorics
Math Challenge III Combinatorics
Math Challenge I-A Number Theory
Math Challenge I-B Number Theory
Math Challenge I-C Finite Math
Math Challenge II-A Number Theory
Math Challenge II-B Number Theory
Math Challenge III Number Theory

COMING SOON FROM ARETEEM PRESS

Fun Math Problem Solving For Elementary School Vol. 2 (and Solutions Manual)
Counting & Probability for Middle School (and Solutions Manual) - From Common Core to Math Competitions
Number Theory Problem Solving for Middle School (and Solutions Manual) - From Common Core to Math Competitions

The books are available in paperback and eBook formats (including Kindle and other formats).
To order the books, visit `https://areteem.org/bookstore`.

Contents

Introduction 7

1 ZIML Contests 15
- 1.1 October 2018 17
- 1.2 November 2018 25
- 1.3 December 2018 35
- 1.4 January 2019 43
- 1.5 February 2019 51
- 1.6 March 2019 59
- 1.7 April 2019 67
- 1.8 May 2019 75
- 1.9 June 2019 83

2 ZIML Solutions 91
- 2.1 October 2018 92
- 2.2 November 2018 101
- 2.3 December 2018 110
- 2.4 January 2019 119
- 2.5 February 2019 128

Copyright © ARETEEM INSTITUTE. All rights reserved.

2.6	March 2019	139
2.7	April 2019	149
2.8	May 2019	157
2.9	June 2019	166
3	**Appendix**	**175**
3.1	Division M Topics Covered	175
3.2	Glossary of Common Math Terms	179
3.3	ZIML Answers	186

Introduction

Each month during the school year, Areteem Institute hosts the online Zoom International Math League (ZIML) competitions. Students can compete in one of five divisions based on their age and mathematical level (details shown on Page 9).

This book contains the problems, answers, and full solutions from the nine ZIML Division M Competitions held during the 2018-2019 School Year. It is divided into three parts:

1. The complete Division M ZIML Competitions (20 questions per competition) from October 2018 to June 2019.
2. The solutions for each of the competitions, including detailed work and helpful tricks.
3. An appendix including the topics and knowledge points covered for Division M, a glossary including common mathematical terms, and answer keys for each of the competitions so students can easily check their work.

The questions found on the ZIML competitions are meant to test your problem solving skills and train you to apply the knowledge you know to many different applications. We hope you enjoy the problems!

Copyright © ARETEEM INSTITUTE. All rights reserved.

Introduction

About Zoom International Math League

The Zoom International Math League (ZIML) has a simple goal: provide a platform for students to build and share their passion for math and other STEM fields with students from around the globe. Started in 2008 as the Southern California Mathematical Olympiad, ZIML has a rich history of past participants who have advanced to top tier colleges and prestigious math competitions, including American Math Competitions, MATHCOUNTS, and the International Math Olympaid.

The ZIML Core Online Programs, most available with a free account at `ziml.areteem.org`, include:

- **Daily Magic Spells:** Provides a problem a day (Monday through Friday) for students to practice, with full solutions available the next day.
- **Weekly Brain Potions:** Provides one problem per week posted in the online discussion forum at `ziml.areteem.org`. Usually the problem does not have a simple answer, and students can join the discussion to share their thoughts regarding the scenarios described in the problem, explore the math concepts behind the problem, give solutions, and also ask further questions.
- **Monthly Contests:** The ZIML Monthly Contests are held the first weekend of each month during the school year (October through June). Students can compete in one of 5 divisions to test their knowledge and determine their strengths and weaknesses, with winners announced after the competition.
- **Math Competition Practice:** The Practice page contains sample ZIML contests and an archive of AMC-series tests for online practice. The practices simulate the real contest environment with time-limits of the contests automatically controlled by the server.
- **Online Discussion Forum:** The Online Discussion Forum

Introduction

is open for any comments and questions. Other discussions, such as hard Daily Magic Spells or the Weekly Brain Potions are also posted here.

These programs encourage students to participate consistently, so they can track their progress and improvement each year.

In addition to the online programs, ZIML also hosts onsite Local Tournaments and Workshops in various locations in the United States. Each summer, there are onsite ZIML Competitions at held at Areteem Summer Programs, including the International ZIML Convention, which is a two day convention with one day of workshops and one day of competition.

ZIML Monthly Contests are organized into five divisions ranging from upper elementary school to advanced material based on high school math.

- **Varsity:** This is the top division. It covers material on the level of the last 10 questions on the AMC 12 and AIME level. This division is open to all age levels.
- **Junior Varsity:** This is the second highest competition division. It covers material at the AMC 10/12 level and State and National MathCounts level. This division is open to all age levels.
- **Division H:** This division focuses on material from a standard high school curriculum. It covers topics up to and including pre-calculus. This division will serve as excellent practice for students preparing for the math portions of the SAT or ACT. This division is open to all age levels.
- **Division M:** This division focuses on problem solving using math concepts from a standard middle school math curriculum. It covers material at the level of AMC 8 and School or Chapter MathCounts. This division is open to all students who have not started grade 9.

- **Division E:** This division focuses on advanced problem solving with mathematical concepts from upper elementary school. It covers material at a level comparable to MOEMS Division E. This division is open to all students who have not started grade 6.

This problem book features the Division M Contests. For a detailed list of topics covered for Division M see p.175 in the Appendix.

To participate in the ZIML Online Programs, create a free account at ziml.areteem.org. The ZIML site features are also provided on the ZIML Mobile App, which is available for download from Apple's App Store and Google Play Store.

Introduction

About Areteem Institute

Areteem Institute is an educational institution that develops and provides in-depth and advanced math and science programs for K-12 (Elementary School, Middle School, and High School) students and teachers. Areteem programs are accredited supplementary programs by the Western Association of Schools and Colleges (WASC). Students may attend the Areteem Institute in one or more of the following options:

- Live and real-time face-to-face online classes with audio, video, interactive online whiteboard, and text chatting capabilities;
- Self-paced classes by watching the recordings of the live classes;
- Short video courses for trending math, science, technology, engineering, English, and social studies topics;
- Summer Intensive Camps held on prestigious university campuses and Winter Boot Camps;
- Practice with selected free daily problems and monthly ZIML competitions at `ziml.areteem.org`.

Areteem courses are designed and developed by educational experts and industry professionals to bring real world applications into STEM education. The programs are ideal for students who wish to build their mathematical strength in order to excel academically and eventually win in Math Competitions (AMC, AIME, USAMO, IMO, ARML, MathCounts, Math Olympiad, ZIML, and other math leagues and tournaments, etc.), Science Fairs (County Science Fairs, State Science Fairs, national programs like Intel Science and Engineering Fair, etc.) and Science Olympiads, or for students who purely want to enrich their academic lives by taking more challenging courses and developing outstanding analytical, logical, and creative problem solving skills.

Since 2004 Areteem Institute has been teaching with methodology that is highly promoted by the new Common Core State Standards: stressing the conceptual level understanding of the math concepts, problem solving techniques, and solving problems with real world applications. With the guidance from experienced and passionate professors, students are motivated to explore concepts deeper by identifying an interesting problem, researching it, analyzing it, and using a critical thinking approach to come up with multiple solutions.

Thousands of math students who have been trained at Areteem have achieved top honors and earned top awards in major national and international math competitions, including Gold Medalists in the International Math Olympiad (IMO), top winners and qualifiers at the USA Math Olympiad (USAMO/JMO) and AIME, top winners at the Zoom International Math League (ZIML), and top winners at the MathCounts National Competition. Many Areteem Alumni have graduated from high school and gone on to enter their dream colleges such as MIT, Cal Tech, Harvard, Stanford, Yale, Princeton, U Penn, Harvey Mudd College, UC Berkeley, or UCLA. Those who have graduated from colleges are now playing important roles in their fields of endeavor.

Further information about Areteem Institute, as well as updates and errata of this book, can be found online at `http://www.areteem.org`.

Introduction

Acknowledgments

This book contains the Online ZIML Division M Problems from the 2018-19 school year. These problems were created and compiled by the staff of Areteem Institute. These problems were inspired by questions from the Areteem Math Challenge Courses, past questions on the ACT/SAT/GRE, past math competitions, math textbooks, and countless other resources and people encountered by the Areteem Curriculum Department in their life devoted to math. We thank all these sources for growing and nurturing our passion for math.

The Areteem staff, including John Lensmire, David Reynoso, Kevin Wang, and Kelly Ren, are the main contributors who compiled, edited, and reviewed this book.

Lastly, thanks to all the students who have participated and continue to participate in the Zoom International Math League. Your dedication to the Daily Magic Spells and Monthly Contests makes all of this possible, and we hope you continue to enjoy ZIML for years to come!

1. ZIML Contests

This part of the book contains the Division M ZIML Contests from the 2018-19 School Year. There were nine monthly competitions, held on the dates found below:

- October 5-7
- November 2-4
- December 7-9
- January 4-6
- February 1-3
- March 1-3
- April 5-7
- May 3-5
- June 7-9

1.1 ZIML October 2018 Division M

Below are the 20 Problems from the Division M ZIML Competition held in October 2018.
The answer key is available on p.186 in the Appendix.
Full solutions to these questions are available starting on p.92.

Problem 1
Luke was reading a Shakespeare book for his English class and an Evolution book for his Biology class. Every day he would read $\frac{1}{9}$ of the Shakespeare book and then $\frac{1}{5}$ of the Evolution book. The Shakespeare book was 297 pages long, and the Evolution book was 395 pages long. If he started reading both books on the same day, how many pages does he have left on the Shakespeare book after he finishes reading the Evolution book?

Problem 2
A number $\overline{a2a4a6a}$ is divisible by 33. What is the sum of all possible values of a?

Problem 3
At the pet farm there are dogs, cats and monkeys. Andy counted 89 heads and 282 legs altogether. If there are three times as many dogs as cats in the pet farm, how many dogs are there?

Problem 4
Several squares are arranged to form a rectangle like in the diagram below.

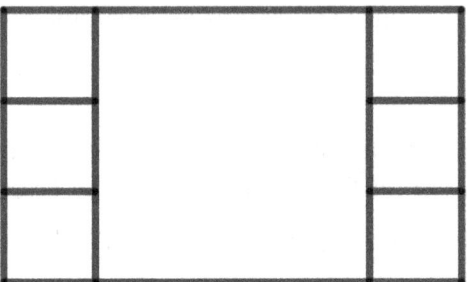

If the area of the big square is 20 more square units than the area of 4 small squares combined, what is the perimeter of the big rectangle?

Problem 5
After the pirates went to hunt for treasure they decided to divide the coins they collected evenly. When they tried to divide the coins amongst all pirates, there were 5 coins left over so they threw one pirate off the ship and tried again, this time having 2 coins left over. If there were originally 9 pirates in the group, what is the smallest possible number of coins for which this could have happened?

Problem 6
Summer collects old used pens, either black or blue. She currently has 342 pens, and if she had 23 more blue pens and 9 less black pens, she would have three times as many black pens as blue pens. How many blue pens does Summer have?

Problem 7
Consider the following diagram, where the circle has radius 6 and $\widehat{AB}$ is an arc of $120°$.

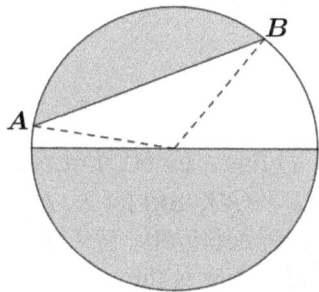

The area of the shaded region is $A \times \pi + B \times \sqrt{3}$. What is $A + B$?

Problem 8
What is the smallest multiple of 25 that has exactly 10 factors?

Problem 9
Lisha can wash a huge pile of dishes in 6 hours. Brandee can wash the same pile of dishes in 4 hours. Lisha washes dishes for 2 hours and then Brandee comes to help her. How many hours did Lisha wash dishes?

Problem 10
Danny had a stack of 10 cards with the numbers 1 through 10. He randomly picks two cards and multiplies the numbers that he gets. The probability that he gets an even number is $P\%$. What is P? Round your answer to the nearest tenth.

Problem 11
Parallelogram $ABCD$ has area 60. Let G and H be points on DC such that $CF = FG = GD$, and let E, H and I be the midpoints of AB, BC and DA, respectively. If J, K are the intersections of EF and EG with IH, what is the area of $\triangle EKJ$, rounded to the nearest tenth.

Problem 12
Let a, b and c be such that $\gcd(a,b,c) = 10$ and $\text{lcm}(a,b,c) = 600$. If $\text{lcm}(a,b) = 40$, what is the smallest possible value of c that we could have?

1.1 ZIML October 2018 Division M

Problem 13
Caprice loves to have a variety of car air fresheners available. She is at the store and wants to buy a collection (in no particular order) of 6 car air fresheners (that should last her a good two months). There are 5 different scents available. In how many different ways can she choose which ones to buy?

Problem 14
At Linguine's italian restaurant they can serve an average of 24 hungry customers every 15 minutes. At Tacos Don Julio, they can serve an average of 52 hungry customers every 10 minutes. A group of 153 hungry customers splits in two groups, one that goes to Linguine's and one that goes to Tacos Don Julio. Both groups finish being served at the same time. How many hungry customers ate at Tacos Don Julio?

Problem 15
Ben just came back from trick-or-treating. He scored 15 special candies that he placed in a separate bag to enjoy later. There were 7 chocolates, 4 bags of gummies, and 4 packs of gum. If he randomly grabs two items from his special candy bag the probability that he grabs two different kinds of candy is $\frac{P}{Q}$ as a reduced fraction. What is $Q - P$?

Problem 16
Sally is going to have a tea party in her room. All the bears and Barbies are invited. There are 4 bears and 7 Barbie's attending the tea party, and they will all seat around a circular table. Some of the bears recently got into an argument, so Sally wants to make sure no two bears sit next to each other. Sally will be serving the tea, so she will not be sitting at the table. If all chair are identical, in how many different ways can the bears and Barbie's sit for the tea party?

Problem 17
Consider equilateral triangle ABC, square $ACED$, regular pentagon $ADHGF$ and regular hexagon $AFLKJI$ as in the diagram below.

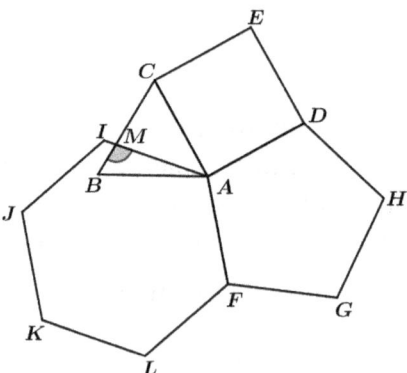

How many degrees is the angle measure of $\angle AMB$?

Problem 18
Two parallelograms are drawn on the sides of a rhombus of side length 10, like in the diagram below.

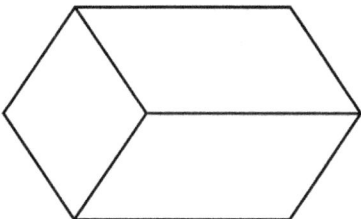

If the larger diagonal of the rhombus has length 16 and the longer side of he parallelograms have length 17, what is the area of the whole figure?

Problem 19
What is the remainder when dividing $2018^{2018} \times 2019^{2019}$ by 7?

Problem 20
Jeff ordered a new video game on an online store, which is supposed to arrive to his house some time between 7 : 00 AM and 11 : 00 AM. He has to go to work, and his carpool buddy is picking him up some time between 8 : 00 AM and 9 : 00 AM. They will leave as soon as he comes to pick him up. The probability that Jeff receives his new video game before he has to leave for work is $\dfrac{P}{Q}$ as a reduced fraction. What is $Q - P$?

1.2 ZIML November 2018 Division M

Below are the 20 Problems from the Division M ZIML Competition held in November 2018.
The answer key is available on p.187 in the Appendix.
Full solutions to these questions are available starting on p.101.

Problem 1
In the following diagram the squares have side length 3 and 5.

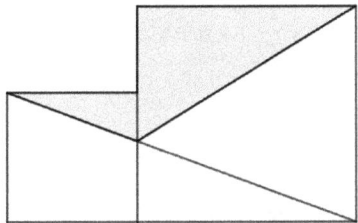

What is the area of the shaded region? Round your answer to the nearest tenth.

Problem 2
A group of 5 worker ants can build a bridge in half a day.

If 30 ants work together, how many hours do they need to finish the job?

Problem 3

Albert, Bertha, and Carl agree to meet for lunch. They arrive separately at the restaurant at a random time between 12:00 PM and 1:00 PM.

It is restaurant policy that they can't be seated at their table until all members of a party arrive. The restaurant serves a super special lunch menu that guests can order only if they were seated at their tables before 12:30 PM.

The probability that Albert and his friends can order the super special lunch menu is $\dfrac{P}{Q}$ as a reduced fraction. What is $Q - P$?

Problem 4

Consider two integers a and b, where a is a perfect square, $\gcd(a,b) = 72$ and $\operatorname{lcm}(a,b) = 43200$.

What is the largest possible value of b?

Problem 5

Mr. Rivers finished grading 13 assignments and found the average grade his students obtained was 82 points. Two more students turned in the assignment late, but since they raised the average grade to 83 points, Mr. Rivers accepted them.

If the grades of this two assignments were 7 points apart, what was the grade in the assignment with the lower grade?

Problem 6
What is the largest 4-digit multiple of 66 and 78 that has two different digits? (For example, 1234 is has 4 different digits, while 1221 has 2 different digits.)

Problem 7
In the following diagram (not to scale), triangles $\triangle AFJ$, $\triangle BGF$, and $\triangle CHG$ are isosceles. (The diagram does correctly tell us, for example, that $\angle AFJ = \angle AJF$.)

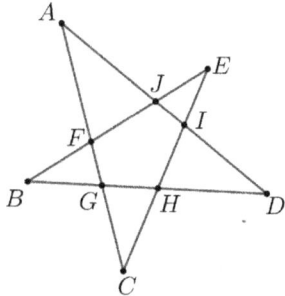

Problem 8
Larry was trying to get ready for his swimming season, so he started doing sit ups at home on October 1st.

He started with 24 sit ups the first day, and increased the number of sit ups he did each day by 5. He did this each day until October 31st. How many sit ups did Larry do in total?

Problem 9
Mr. Furn E. Ture and 2 of his workers can build 5 dining tables in one week. A big retailer is asking them to build 50 dining tables in two weeks.

How many additional workers would Mr. Furn E. Ture need to hire to be able to finish the job in time? (Assume Mr. Furn E. Ture, his current workers and any new workers can all work at the same pace.)

Problem 10
Find the largest 4-digit number that leaves a remainder of 4 when divided by 5 and a remainder of 5 when divided by 6.

Problem 11
Isadora needs to buy some crayons for an art project. She bought some packs of 10 crayons that cost $2.50 and some packs of 15 crayons that cost $3.50.

If she bought a total of 160 crayons in 13 packs, how many dollars did she spend?

Problem 12

In the following diagram $ABCD$ is a trapezoid with bases 2 and 8, and area 15.

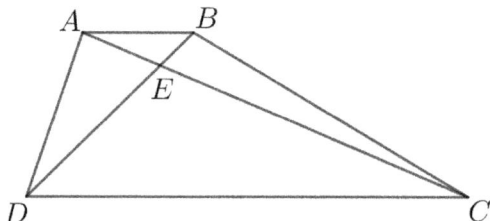

If $AE : EC = 1 : 4$, what is the area of $\triangle ABE$? Round your answer to the nearest tenth.

Problem 13

Erika chooses a first, second, third, and fourth number randomly from the integers $1, 2, \ldots, 10$. (It is possible for Erika to choose the same number multiple times.)

The probability that Erika's four numbers add up to 10 can be written as $\dfrac{P}{Q}$ as a reduced fraction. What is $Q - P$?

Problem 14

Lizzie made herself a cup of coffee that was 80% coffee and 20% milk. She drank half of it and then forgot about it.

Later in the day she grabbed her cup, filled it to the top with hot coffee, and drank only half of it.

At night, she grabbed her cup once more and this time filled it to the top with milk.

Now $P\%$ of her cup is coffee. What is P? Round your answer to the nearest tenth.

Problem 15

In the following diagram there is a rhombus with side length 12 and an angle of $120°$, and a semicircle whose diamter has the same length as the minor diagonal of the rhombus.

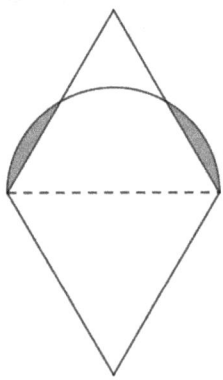

The shaded region has area $A \times \sqrt{B} + C \times \pi$, where A, B and C are integers, and B has no square factors. What is $A + B - C$?

Problem 16
Line segment *CD* is tangent to the circle shown below at *B*, with *A* the center of the circle.

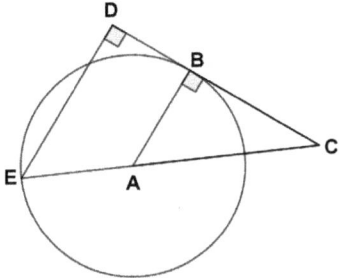

If △*ABC* has sides *AB* = 3 and *BC* = 4, the area of △*CDE* can be written as a reduced fraction $\frac{P}{Q}$. What is $P + Q$?

Problem 17
Sibyl is arranging some chess pieces in a circle. She has 6 white pawns, 2 white rooks, 2 white bishops, 1 black pawn and 1 black rook.

In how many different ways can she arrange the chess pieces if she wants to make sure the two black pieces are not adjacent to each other?

Problem 18

Tiffani collects stamps. If she had 4 more super hero stamps, she'd have three times as many super hero stamps as space stamps. And if she had 7 fewer super hero stamps, she'd have the same number of super hero stamps and Cinderella stamps.

If Tiffani has 209 stamps in total, how many Cinderella stamps does she have?

Problem 19

At Primrose's Halloween party everyone gets a number to participate in the costume contest.

The theme for the party was Ghosts vs. Werewolves, so everyone came as a ghost or a werewolf.

Primrose gave everyone a different number that was a factor of 1400. Ghosts all got even numbers, werewolves all got odd numbers, and Primrose gave away all factors of 1400.

In the first round of the costume contest, Primrose paired 1 with 1400, 2 with 700, 4 with 350, etc. Everyone at the party voted for their favorite costume in each pair, and winners advanced to the next round.

Regardless of how good their costumes were, if a ghost was competing against a werewolf, all ghosts voted for the ghost and all werewolves voted for the werewolf.

How many ghosts advanced to the second round?

Problem 20
What is the remainder of $1 + 2^2 + 3^3 + 4^4 + \cdots + 22^{22}$ when divided by 4?

1.3 ZIML December 2018 Division M

Below are the 20 Problems from the Division M ZIML Competition held in December 2018.
The answer key is available on p.188 in the Appendix.
Full solutions to these questions are available starting on p.110.

Problem 1
Mr. Smith's computer messed up one problem on his exam about sequences. It printed the sequence

$$3, 3\star 2, 3\star 2\star 2, 3\star 2\star 2\star 2, \ldots$$

and asked students to find the 10th term in the sequence. Some students thought $\star = \times$ and got an answer G. Others thought $\star = +$ and got an answer A. What is $G - A$?

Problem 2
George has cubes of volume 1, 8, 27, and 64. He stacks them and glues them to make a tower as shown below.

What is the surface area of this solid? Round your answer to the nearest integer.

Problem 3
Consider the 37 digit number

$$373737\cdots 3$$

where the digits alternate between 3 and 7. What is the remainder when this number is divided by 9?

Problem 4
Everyday Pat spends 30 minutes walking to school and 45 minutes on his way back home, since he is not in a rush to come back.

If his average speed on the round trip is 3.5 miles per hour, what is the distance, in miles, from his house to the school? Round your answer to the nearest tenth of a mile.

Problem 5
How many of the fractions

$$\frac{1}{2}, \frac{2}{4}, \frac{3}{8}, \ldots, \frac{10}{1024}$$

are irreducible?

Problem 6

A star is drawn by connecting diagonals in a regular pentagon as shown below.

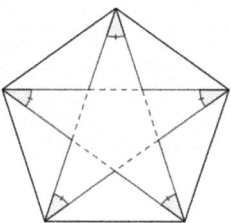

Each of the five marked angles have a measure of $K°$. What is K, rounded to the nearest integer?

Problem 7

Ms. Winterspoon asked her students to choose which of Chocolate, Strawberry, or Vanilla was their favorite flavor for ice cream. She summarized the results of the poll in the following chart:

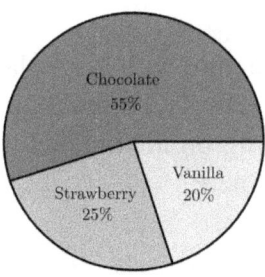

If there were 20 students that chose Strawberry as their favorite flavor, how many people chose Chocolate?

Problem 8
Consider the data collected in the frequency table below.

#	1	2	3	4	5	6	7	8	9	10
Freq.	0	2	0	1	0	3	6	4	3	2

Find the mean, median, and mode for this data. What is the sum of all three?

Problem 9
Sally has a bird fountain in her backyard. Birds come all the time to drink water from it. It is big enough that a big bird would take 25 minutes to drink all the water and a small bird would take 50 minutes to drink all the water.

Sally had just filled the water fountain when 2 big birds and 1 small bird came to drink from it. If all 3 birds keep drinking at a steady pace, how long will it take them to drink all the water in the fountain?

Problem 10
Coach Greg took a picture with his 5 player basketball team after they won a tournament. The 6 lined up for the photo. If Coach Greg was not standing on the outside in the picture, how many different photos are there?

Problem 11
The number 2018____ is a multiple of 120, what is the number?

Problem 12
Four semicircles are arranged as in the diagram below.

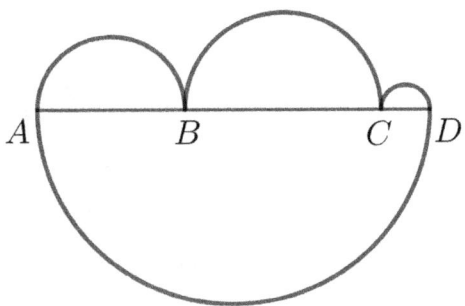

If $AB : BC : CD = 3 : 4 : 1$, and $AD = 24$, the perimeter of the figure is $K \times \pi$. What is K?

Problem 13
A fair six-sided die, numbered $1-6$, is rolled three times. The probability that the sum of the three rolls is 5 can be written as $\frac{P}{Q}$ for positive integers P and Q with $\gcd(P,Q) = 1$. What is $P + Q$?

Problem 14
To get in the holiday spirit, Paul and his little sister Mary bought 50 packs of candy canes. Paul had planned on carrying all the packs, but Mary wanted to help out. In the end, Paul carried 2 more than 3 times the amount Mary carried. How many packs of candy canes did Mary carry?

Problem 15

Several congruent rhombi of side length 1 are arranged to form a parallelogram like in the diagram below.

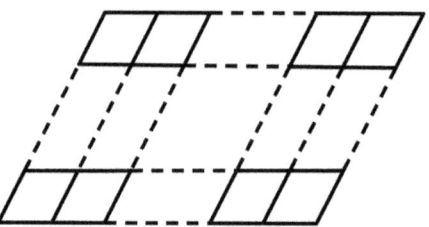

If the perimeter of the resulting parallelogram is 40, and there are the same number of rhombi on each edge of the parallelogram, how many rhombi form the parallelogram?

Problem 16

Jared's phone is programmed to give him an alert each hour, saying for example

$$\text{IT'S NOW 8:00 AM}$$

Unfortunately the clock is off in his phone, so each hour his message is delayed by an additional 5 minutes. For example, if the 8:00 AM alert is correct, Jared will get the

$$\text{IT'S NOW 9:00 AM}$$

alert at 9:05 AM.

Assuming the 8:00 AM alert is correct, how long will it be until Jared gets another correct 8:00 AM alert?

Problem 17
Phil collects decks of cards to play poker with. Some of the decks are standard decks with 52 cards and some other decks include 2 extra cards (the jokers).

Phil has 85 decks of cards in total and 4480 total cards. How many of Phil's decks are standard decks?

Problem 18
Jacob is doing a math puzzle. Right now he needs to find the smallest number N so that N has exactly 16 factors, at least 3 of which must be primes. What is N?

Problem 19
In class, Monty used toothpicks to create a triangle, a square, a pentagon, a hexagon, and an octagon. All the toothpicks were the same, but he labeled which toothpicks he used for each shape. Monty mixed up the toothpicks and chose two of them. The probability the first toothpick Monty chose was from the octagon and the second was from the pentagon can be written as $\dfrac{R}{S}$ for positive integers R, S with $\gcd(R, S) = 1$. What is $S - R$?

Problem 20

In the diagram below, $ABCD$, $DEFA$, $EHIP$ and $CIHG$ are parallelograms, and G and H are the midpoints of CD and DE, respectively.

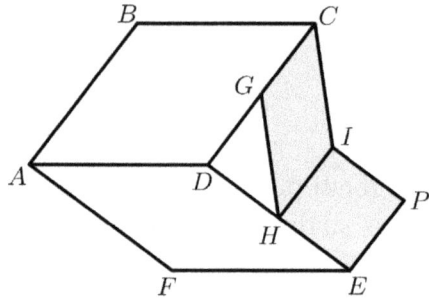

If, $DA = DC = DE = 5$, the area of $ABCD$ is 20, and the area of $DEFA$ is 15, what is the area of the shaded region?

1.4 ZIML January 2019 Division M

Below are the 20 Problems from the Division M ZIML Competition held in January 2019.
The answer key is available on p.189 in the Appendix.
Full solutions to these questions are available starting on p.119.

Problem 1
How many numbers between 100 and 400 (inclusive) are divisible by their hundreds digit?

Problem 2
At The Great Cookie Factory they make three kinds of cookies: Super Duper Chocolate cookies (SDC), Coco-coffee cookies (CC), and Sparkling Sugar cookies (SS). They currently ship their cookies to Cookie-Mart and The Cookie Emporium. The following table summarizes what percent of cookies of each kind were sent to each of the two stores this month:

	SDC	CC	SS
Cookie-Mart	80%	50%	30%
The Cookie Emporium	20%	50%	70%

If Cookie-Mart received 150 boxes of Coco-coffee cookies and 240 boxes of Sparkling Sugar cookies, and The Cookie Emporium received 80 boxes of Super Duper Chocolate cookies, how many boxes of cookies were shipped by The Great Cookie Factory this month?

Problem 3
In the following diagram the vertices of the shaded triangle are the midpoints of the corresponding sides of the trapezoid.

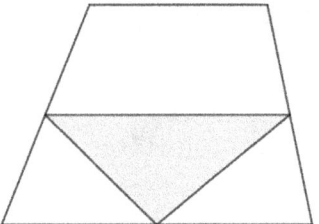

Problem 4
Elmer has three blue cards, five red cards, and four green cards. All cards of the same color are identical. In how many ways can he arrange the cards in a line so that not two red cards are next to each other?

Problem 5
Consider regular octagon $ABCDEFGH$. Extend diagonals $\overline{AC}$ and $\overline{DF}$ and label their intersection J. Find the measure of $\angle AJF$ in degrees. Round your answer to the nearest tenth.

Problem 6

Alex, Brittany, and Celeste are painting their apartment walls. If Alex painted the walls by himself, he would take 16 hours to finish the job. If Brittany painted the walls by herself, she would take 32 hours to finish the job. If Celeste painted the walls by herself, she would also take 32 hours to finish the job.

Alex and Celeste work together for 8 hours, and then Brittany joins them to finish the job.

How many hours did Brittany work?

Problem 7

Consider the following diagram with a square of side length 6 and a square of side length 2.

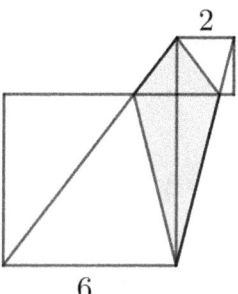

What is the area of the shaded region?

Problem 8
Cammie wrote the letters of the word

| T | O | T | T | O | F | O | L | L |

in separate cards. How many different 9-letter words can she make with the cards? (Note: The words may not be real words in English.)

Problem 9
In Ms. Johnson's class, the ratio of the number of boys that like dogs to the number of boys that like cats is 7 : 3, and the ratio of the number of girls that like dogs to the number of girls that like cats is 4 : 5 (all students like dogs or cats, and no student likes both).

If the ratio of boys to girls in Ms. Johnson's class is 5 : 9, what is the least number of students that could be in Ms. Johnson's class?

Problem 10
Find the smallest number that is a multiple of 21 and has exactly 21 factors.

Problem 11
Jossie has a bag with seven green balls, four red balls, and one blue ball. She then grabs two of them at the same time.

The probability that both balls are the same color is $\frac{P}{Q}$ as a fraction in lowest terms. What is $Q - P$?

Problem 12
Ross drew a parallelogram. Then he joined the midpoints of all sides of his parallelogram to form a smaller parallelogram. He then joined the midpoints of the second parallelogram to form a third parallelogram, as shown in the diagram.

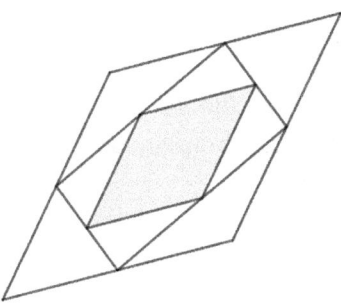

If the smaller parallelogram has area 31, what is the area of the largest parallelogram?

Problem 13
How many different ways are there to sit 6 adults and 3 children at a circular table if we do not want two kids to be sitting next to each other?

Problem 14
Rosabella bought tons of her favorite pens. The glitter inked pens cost $2.50 per pack, and come in packs of 2 pens. The non-glitter inked pens cost $1.50 per pack and come in packs of 3 pens.

She bought 23 packs of pens and got 54 pens in total. How many dollars did she spend?

Problem 15

On her daily commute to work, Lorraine usually rides her bike to the metro station, then takes the metro, and then rides her bike from the metro to her office.

When she is riding her bike, her average speed is 20 miles per hour. The distance from her house to the metro station is 6 miles, and the distance from the metro station to her office is 4 miles.

If she travels for 1 hour and 40 minutes, and she rides the metro for 35 miles, what is the average speed of the metro train in miles per hour?

Problem 16

Alison, Betty, Chelsea, Danny, Esmeralda, and Fatima play a game of tag. They play according to a special set of rules: (i) they randomly choose the first person to be "it", (ii) they cannot tag someone who has been "it" before, unless everyone else has been "it" already, and (iii) the game ends when someone has been "it" twice.

If they make an ordered list of the names of the people who were "it" during the game, how many possible different lists could they make?

Problem 17

Patricia has a circle with area 16π. William draws two congruent circles inside Patricia's circle that do not overlap (but possibly are tangent). If William draws his circle as large as possible, when $K\%$ of Patricia's circle will be covered. What is K, rounded to the nearest integer?

Problem 18
How many different ways are there to arrange the numbers 1, 2, 3, 4, 5, 6, 7, and 8 in a line so that the sum of every four consecutive numbers is divisible by 4?

Problem 19
What is the largest 5-digit number that starts with 7 and is a multiple of 9?

Problem 20
What is the remainder of $1^1 + 10^{10} + 100^{100} + \cdots + 100000^{100000}$ when it is divided by 11?

1.5 ZIML February 2019 Division M

Below are the 20 Problems from the Division M ZIML Competition held in February 2019.
The answer key is available on p.190 in the Appendix.
Full solutions to these questions are available starting on p.128.

Problem 1
A team of 5 workers can build a house in 2 weeks, working 6 days a week for 8 hours each day.

How many hours would it take a team of 20 workers to build 4 houses?

Problem 2
In the diagram below the smaller squares have area 4.

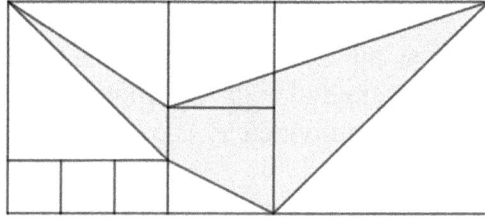

What is the area of the shaded region?

Problem 3
David rented a car for a few days, and was told that he needed to return it with the tank $\frac{3}{4}$ full, as it was when he picked it up.

The car dashboard says that the tank is now half empty. It also says that the car fuel efficiency is 24 miles per gallon, and that he could drive for 168 more miles with the gas remaining in the tank.

How many gallons of gas would David need to buy before he returns the car?

Problem 4
Find the largest 4-digit number of the form 1_3_ that is divisible by 36.

Problem 5
Find the smallest number that leaves a remainder of 7 when divided by 12, a remainder of 11 when divided by 16, and a remainder of 16 when divided by 21.

Problem 6
Isiah is cooking several dishes for his company's potluck. He know some of his coworkers do not like their food to be too spicy, so he is making two kinds of dishes: "not too spicy" with 2 chilies in it, and "spicy" with 5 chilies in it.

If he made 12 dishes, and used 45 chilies in total. How many "spicy" dishes did he make?

Problem 7
Three quarter circles have been drawn to produce the following diagram (the points shown are the centers of the quarter circles).

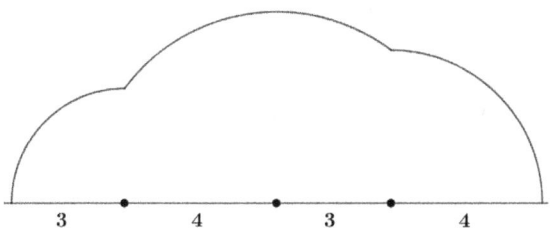

The length of the curve formed by the quarter circles is $\dfrac{P\pi}{Q}$, where P and Q are integers with $\gcd(P, Q) = 1$. What is $P \times Q$?

Problem 8
5 numbers are chosen (possibly with repeats) from the numbers 2, 4, 6, 8, and 10. How many different averages are possible?

Problem 9
How many of the integers $1, 2, \ldots, 100$ are divisible by exactly one of 3, 5, and 11?

Problem 10
How many factors of
$$22^{30} \times 26^{23}$$
are perfect cubes?

Problem 11
Jessee and 7 of her friends decided to travel to Joshua Tree Park for the weekend. Three of them have cars that fit 5 people each, including the driver. The owners of the cars will drive them, and then the rest of them will ride along.

In how many different ways can they choose how many people will ride in each car? (Note: they are only interested in figuring out how many people will ride in each car, not who will be in each car.)

Problem 12
Consider parallelogram $ABCD$. Let E be the midpoint of side AB, F and G be points on side BC such that $BF = FG = GC$, H a point on side CD with $CH = 4HD$, and I the midpoint of DA.

If the area of $ABCD$ is 240, what is the combined area of $\triangle EFG$ and $\triangle EHI$?

Problem 13
James currently has 90 marbles, all either blue, red, or green. Currently the ratio of blue to red to green marbles is $2:3:4$. James buys packs of marbles, each containing 1 red and 2 green marbles, until $\dfrac{1}{18}$ of his marbles are blue. At this point, the ratio of blue to red to green marbles can be written as $P:Q:R$ for positive integers P, Q, and R with $\gcd(P,Q,R) = 1$. What is $P^2 + Q^2 + R^2$?

Problem 14
Aaron randomly picks a number from 0 to 23 (inclusive), and Bert picks a random number from 0 to 59 (inclusive). Then they use their numbers to come up with a time to meet online to play video games with Aaron's number determining the hour and Bert's number determining the minute. For example if Aaron picks 0 and Bert picks 45 they meet at 0:45 or 12:45 AM while if Aaron picks 13 and Bert picks 0 they meet at 13:00 or 1:00 PM.

The probability they agree to meet some time between 6:31 PM and 2:30 AM is $\dfrac{P}{Q}$ as a fraction in lowest terms. What is $Q - P$?

Problem 15
A regular octahedron has surface area $8\sqrt{3}$. What is the sum of the lengths of all edges of the octahedron?

Problem 16
Topanga has 3 numbered red cards, 5 numbered blue cards, and 4 identical black cards.

In how many different ways can Topanga arrange the cards in a circle with no two black cards next to each other?

Problem 17

Robert drove 550 miles to visit his parents over the weekend. On the way, he stopped for gas, snacks, and food. He spent 20 minutes getting gas, 15 minutes getting snacks and 35 minutes getting food.

His GPS kept track of the distance traveled and the time spent traveling, and calculated an average speed of 50 miles per hour for the whole trip.

If he hadn't stopped on the way, what would have been his average speed for the whole trip? Give your answer in mile per hour rounded to the nearest tenth.

Problem 18

Joel wants to play a game at the fair where he has to throw two fair 6-sided dice to decide his prize. The game costs $8 to play, and the player gets as many dollars as the sum of the numbers in the dice.

The probability that Joel wins more money than what he paid for entering the game is $\dfrac{P}{Q}$ as a fraction in lowest terms. What is $P+Q$?

Problem 19
Let $ABCD$ be a concave quadrilateral with $AB = BC = 5$, $CD = DA$, $\angle ABC = 60°$, $\angle BCD = \angle DAB = 30°$, and $\angle CDA = 240°$.

The area of $ABCD$ can be expressed using positive integers P, Q, and R as $\dfrac{P\sqrt{Q}}{R}$, where Q has no square factors and $\gcd(P,R) = 1$. What is $P + Q + R$?

Problem 20
What are the last two digits of
$$15 + 15^2 + 15^3 + \cdots + 15^{10}?$$

1.6 ZIML March 2019 Division M

Below are the 20 Problems from the Division M ZIML Competition held in March 2019.
The answer key is available on p.191 in the Appendix.
Full solutions to these questions are available starting on p.139.

Problem 1
3 workers can decorate 10 cupcakes in 5 minutes. How many minutes would 6 workers need to decorate 200 cupcakes?

Problem 2
Donna has 40 math books in her collection, 15 of which have yellow covers. 22 of her books are geometry books, and the rest cover other topics.

16 of the books do not have yellow covers and are not geometry books. How many of the books are yellow geometry books?

Problem 3
The following diagram shows three semicircles with radii 1, 3, and 4.

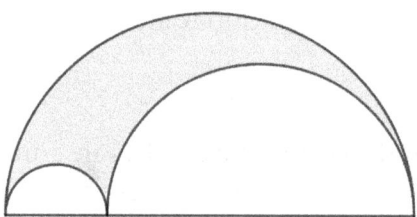

The shaded region has area $K\pi$ for some integer K. What is K?

Problem 4
What is the smallest positive integer that could be added to the list
$$5,5,5,5,5,6,6,6,6,6,6,7,7,7,7,7,7$$
so that the mean of the numbers is greater than the mode (or modes)?

Problem 5
Lois made a huge order of cupcakes at the Cherry Cake bakery. Lois ordered 43 cupcakes, some with 3 cherries on top and some with 5 cherries on top. 3-cherry cupcakes cost $2.50 a piece, and 5-cherry cupcakes cost $3.50 a piece.

If 187 cherries were used for Lois order, how much did she pay?

Problem 6
What is the smallest possible two-digit number that is 27 less than the number obtained by flipping the order of its digits?

Problem 7
Five congruent isosceles triangles are arranged as shown below, with $\overline{AB} \parallel \overline{CD}$.

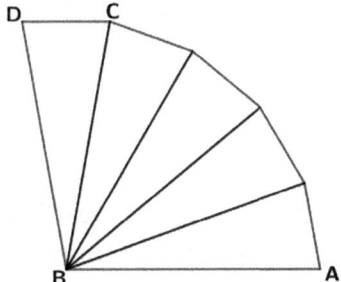

What is the largest angle (measured in degrees) in these triangles? Round your answer to the nearest degree.

Problem 8

Andy is setting up a nice bath for himself. His tub has separate faucets for cold and hot water. The faucet for cold water pours 3 gallons of water per minute. The faucet for hot water pours 5 gallons of water per minute, and can fill the tub in 16 minutes.

Andy opened both faucets and, after 8 minutes, he noticed the drain of the tub was left open.

If 3 gallons of water go down the drain every minute, after closing the drain, how many more minutes would Andy need to leave both faucets open to fill the tub completely?

Problem 9

Liam rolls a fair six-sided die 3 times. If the die is numbered 1, 2, up to 6, the probability that each time he gets a number greater than 2 can be expressed as $\frac{P}{Q}$ for positive integers P and Q with $\gcd(P, Q) = 1$. What is $Q - P$?

Problem 10

Mary is about to eat a salad and wants to add some vinaigrette to it. She has two jars in her fridge with some leftovers from before. One of the jars has 3 ounces of vinaigrette, and she made it by mixing vinegar and olive oil in a 1 : 3 ratio. The other jar has 6 ounces of vinaigrette, which she made by mixing vinegar and olive oil in a 2 : 3 ratio.

Mary decided to mix the contents of both jars before adding the vinaigrette to her salad. The ratio of vinegar and olive oil in this new vinaigrette is $a : b$, with $\gcd(a, b) = 1$. What is $a + b$?

Problem 11
What is the largest three-digit number that leaves a remainder of 2 when divided by 3, a remainder of 2 when divided by 4, and a remainder of 2 when divided by 5?

Problem 12
Let $ABCD$ be a trapezoid with AB parallel to CD, $AB = 8$, $CD = 4$, and height 4. Let M be the midpoint of AB, N be the midpoint of BC and O be the intersection of the diagonals AC and BD.

What is the area of $\triangle MON$?

Problem 13
Russell and Paul were playing tag in a huge open field. Paul started running away from Russell at a rate of 8 m/s. 3 seconds later, Russell started chasing Paul at a rate of 9.5 m/s. When Russell catches up to Paul, how many meters will each have run? Round your answer to the nearest tenth.

Problem 14
How many factors does $11^3 - 7^3$ have?

Problem 15
Dan has 3 blue cards, 4 red cards, and 3 yellow cards. All cards have different symbols on them.

In how many different ways could Dan pick two cards that are different colors?

Problem 16
Find the sum of all six-digit numbers of the form $\overline{a2019b}$ that are divisible by 45.

Problem 17
Percy, the dog, is on a leash tied to a tree in the park. There are two small fences connecting two other trees to the tree where Percy is tied that form an angle of 30°, as pictured on the diagram below.

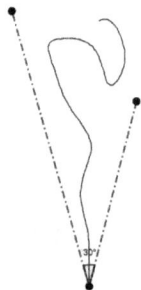

The area where Percy can run freely is $\dfrac{A}{B}\pi$ feet, for some positive integers A and B, with $\gcd(A,B) = 1$. What is $A+B$?

Problem 18

Lacey and some of her friends sit around a circular table and take turns saying numbers out loud clockwise around the circle. Lacey starts by saying 1, and the next person says 1 as well. After that, each person adds up the previous two numbers and then says the remainder when divided by 3 out loud.

After a few rounds they notice they all have been repeating the first number they said. If there are more than 10 people seated at the table, what is the least number of people seated at the table?

Problem 19

Justin got 4 quarters to buy candy at a vending machine. There are 5 different candies to choose from that cost 25 cents and chocolate bars that cost 50 cents.

In how many different ways could Justin choose what to buy if he uses all of his quarters?

Problem 20
In the following diagram all circles have radius 1.

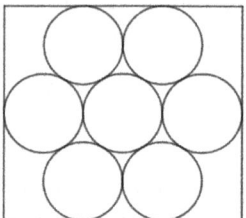

The area of the rectangle is $A + B\sqrt{C}$, for integers A, B, and C, where C does not have any perfect squares (greater than 1) as factors. What is $A + B + C$?

1.7 ZIML April 2019 Division M

Below are the 20 Problems from the Division M ZIML Competition held in April 2019.
The answer key is available on p.192 in the Appendix.
Full solutions to these questions are available starting on p.149.

Problem 1
Richard is writing a new novel. He wrote 10 pages each day for 3 days, and 15 pages each day for 4 days. If he works for an additional 5 days, how many pages would he need to write each day to average 20 pages per day for the entire time?

Problem 2
Among the numbers 71, 73, 75, 77, and 79, which one has the greatest number of factors?

Problem 3
Lisa loves chocolate, so she was shocked when she found out that more than 70% of her classmates do not like chocolate. If Lisa has 32 classmates, what is the least number of people in her class that do not like chocolate?

Problem 4

Jennie bought a crystal sculpture in the shape of a square pyramid. It was packed in a rectangular box with the same base as the pyramid, and just as high as the pyramid. To protect the sculpture, Styrofoam cushioning was added to the package, filling completely all gaps between the box and the pyramid.

If the volume of the pyramid is 15 cubic inches, what is the volume, in cubic inches, of the Styrofoam cushioning?

Problem 5

The least common multiple of two numbers is 144, and their greatest common divisor is 24. If one of the numbers is 48, what is the other number?

Problem 6

ReFresh sparkling water is sold in packs of 4, 8, and 24 bottles. What is the least number of packs that one would need to buy in order to get exactly 92 bottles of sparkling water?

Problem 7

Carly ate 19 pizzas last month. She only ate pepperoni and veggie pizzas. If she had eaten 2 more pepperoni pizzas, she would have eaten twice as many veggie pizzas as pepperoni pizzas.

How many veggie pizzas did Carly eat last month?

Problem 8
A number sequence is such that each term, except for the first two, is the sum of the previous two terms. The fifth term is 26, the sixth term is 42, and the seventh term is 68.

What is the sum of the first two terms of the sequence?

Problem 9
A fair 4-sided die with numbers 2, 3, 5, and 7 is thrown. The probability that the sum of the numbers on the visible faces is a multiple of 4 is $\dfrac{P}{Q}$ as a fraction in lowest terms. What is $Q - P$?

Problem 10
Alan, Beatrice, and Charlie meet up for dinner at a fancy restaurant. They will share two different appetizers, and each will order a different entree so they can all have a bite of each others' meal. On the menu there are 6 appetizers and 8 entrees to choose from. In how many different ways can they choose to order their food?

Problem 11
What is the smallest possible value of K such that $\sqrt{1350 \times K}$ is a perfect square?

Problem 12
Consider the following diagram where a regular hexagon and a regular nonagon share one side.

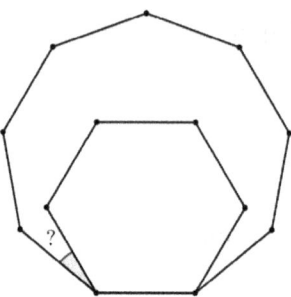

What is the measure of the marked angle in degrees?

Problem 13
Patrick has a carton of orange juice of 16 ounces that is 75% real orange juice, and a carton that is 10 ounces and is 90% real orange juice.

He mixes the whole contents of both cartons of juice, and now $P\%$ of the mix is real orange juice. What is P? Round your answer to the nearest integer.

Problem 14
A four-digit number $\overline{a34b}$ is divisible by 15. What is the smallest possible value for the digit a?

Problem 15
Regina has a box that can hold up to 250 marbles. She then finds a box that is twice as long, twice as wide, and three times as high as her box. How many marbles could this box hold when it is completely full?

Problem 16
How many numbers between 1 and 200 (inclusive) are multiples of 2 and 3, but not 5?

Problem 17
Three 45-45-90 triangles and one 30-60-90 triangle are arranged as in the diagram below.

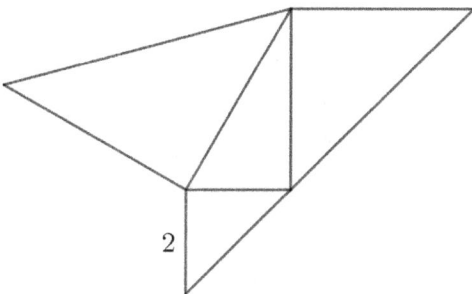

If the legs of the smallest 45-45-90 triangle have length 2, the area of the whole figure is $A + B\sqrt{C}$, for integers A, B, and C, where C has no square factors greater than 1. What is $A + B + C$?

Problem 18

The route 15xps bus is an express route, so it only takes on new passengers at the beginning of its route. After picking up the passengers there are only 6 stops. The bus driver needs to keep track of how many people get off at each of the stops, so he makes an ordered list with the number of people that leave the bus in each of the 6 stops.

If 12 passengers board the bus, how many different lists could the bus driver make?

Problem 19

Eight identical cubes with side length 3 are glued together to produce the figure below. (All of the faces match up when they are glued.)

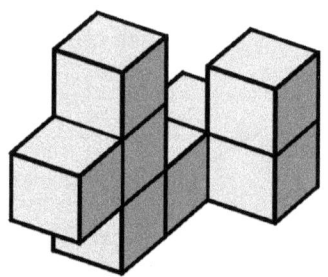

What is the surface area of the whole figure?

Problem 20

Nine consecutive positive integers are arranged in a 3×3 grid so that every row, column, and diagonal have the same sum. Then the numbers are replaced by their remainders when divided by 5, resulting in the following arrangement

0	3	3
0	2	4
1	1	4

What is the least possible value for the sum of the original numbers in each row, column, and diagonal?

1.8 ZIML May 2019 Division M

Below are the 20 Problems from the Division M ZIML Competition held in May 2019.
The answer key is available on p.193 in the Appendix.
Full solutions to these questions are available starting on p.157.

Problem 1
Aiden just ate some green and purple grapes. If he had eaten 10 more green grapes he would have eaten 5 times as many green grapes as purple grapes.

If Aiden ate 98 grapes in total, how many purple grapes did he eat?

Problem 2
In the following diagram $ABCDE$, $AEFGH$, and $AHIJK$ are regular pentagons.

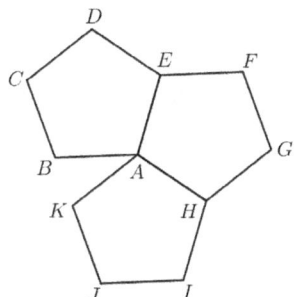

What is the measure of $\angle ICG$? Give your answer in degrees rounded to the nearest tenth.

Problem 3
What is the smallest perfect square that is a multiple of both 15 and 18? (Recall a perfect square is a number that is equal to the square of an integer, for example 4 and 9 are perfect squares).

Problem 4
Ashley did 5 sit ups on Sunday. Each of the following days she did two more sit ups than the previous day. If she continues in this manner, how many sit ups will she do (in total) in two full weeks?

Problem 5
Dawson has 3 green, 4 blue, and 5 red cards. All cards of the same color are identical. If Dawson picks two of the cards at random, the probability that they come of different colors is $\frac{P}{Q}$ as a fraction in lowest terms. What is $Q - P$?

Problem 6
Lance serves himself a (full) cup of coffee that is $\frac{3}{4}$ coffee and $\frac{1}{4}$ milk. After he drinks $\frac{1}{2}$ of his cup, he fills it to the top with coffee and stirs it well.

Now the coffee to milk ratio in his cup is $a : b$, with a and b integers such that $\gcd(a,b) = 1$. What is $a \times b$?

Problem 7

When Dante a shared a brand new bag of candy with his friends, giving each friend the same number of candies, he had 6 candies left over.

The next day one of his friends was not there. He once again shared a brand new bag of candy (the same as the one from the previous day) with his friends, and this time had no candies left over.

If a brand new bag comes with more than 20 but less than 30 candies, how many candies are in the bag?

Problem 8

Roy usually spends 50 minutes folding all of his clothes after his weekly round of laundry. Scottie came to visit Roy to take him out for dinner while he was folding his clothes. Since Scottie was hungry and Roy still had half of his laundry to fold, he decided to jump in and help Roy finish folding his clothes.

If they were done folding Roy's clothes 15 minutes after Scottie started helping, how much time would it have taken Scottie to fold all of Roy's clothes by himself? Give your answer in minutes rounded to the nearest whole minute.

Problem 9

The figure below is made up of 5 squares and two isosceles right triangles.

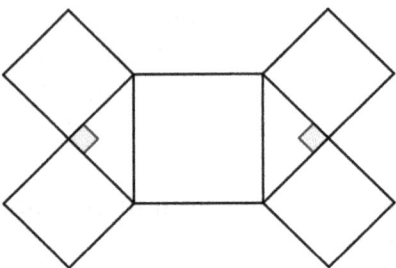

If the left isosceles right triangle has an area of 8, what is the combined area of the entire figure?

Problem 10

Lisa and Anthony run on a circular track at the same constant speed. They start running at diametrically opposite points on the track in opposite directions. They meet for the first time after they each have run 150 meters.

What distance would they each have run in total when they meet for the 5th time on the track? Give your answer in meters rounded to the nearest integer.

Problem 11

In the diagram below the three circles have radius 4 and contain the centers of the other two circles.

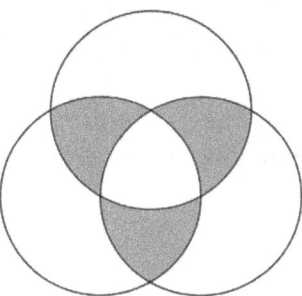

The shaded region has area $K \times \pi$ for some integer K. What is K?

Problem 12

Ms. Keaton has 10 numbered cards: $2, 3, 4, \ldots, 11$. She gave each of her 10 students one of the cards and asked them to form groups based on the number of factors their number had (so all students with a card with a number with 2 factors would be on the same group, etc.).

How many groups did her students make?

Problem 13
Russ works as a cashier at the entrance of one of the local beach parking lots. Today 51 vehicles entered the parking lot during Russ's shift. The fee for entering the parking lot is $15 for a regular vehicle and $20 if the vehicle is towing a 2 wheel trailer. All other vehicles must park at alternate locations.

If Russ counted 230 wheels entering the parking lot during his shift, how much money did he receive from people parking at his parking lot?

Problem 14
Stacey and Tracy start walking from the same point. Stacey walks 24 meters north and Tracy walks 18 meters east. How far apart from each other are they now? Give your answer in meters rounded to the nearest tenth.

Problem 15
A 6-sided die with numbers $1, \ldots, 6$ is such that the probability of getting 1 is 20%, the probability of getting 3 is 30%, the probability of getting 5 is 25%, and 2, 4, and 6 are equally likely to occur.

If someone rolls the die, the probability that the result is prime is P%. What is P? Round your answer to the nearest tenth.

Problem 16
Let A, B and C be integers such that $\gcd(A,B) = 20$, $\gcd(B,C) = 6$, and $\text{lcm}(A,C) = 1800$. What is the smallest possible value of C?

Problem 17

Three families went hiking and want to take a group photo with all of them together: the Spears (mom, dad, and two kids), the Atkinsons (mom and two kids), and the Lockwoods (mom, dad, and one kid).

If they want each of the families to stand together in a line for the picture, in how many different ways can they be arranged for the photo?

Problem 18

Two square pyramids are drawn in a rectangular prism with dimensions $6 \times 4 \times 2$ as shown in the diagram below.

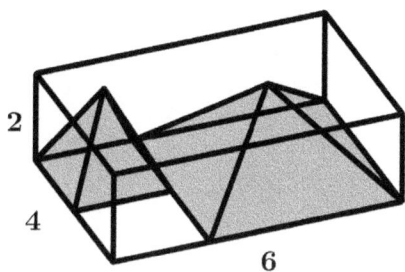

Both pyramids have the same height as the prism, but one of the pyramids has a base side length that is twice the other. What is the combined volume of the two pyramids? Round your answer to the nearest tenth.

Problem 19

What is the smallest positive integer n that makes $\dfrac{\sqrt{12n}}{14}$ a perfect square?

Problem 20

As part of a class survey 32 students were asked if they had cats, dogs, or hamsters as pets at home.

11 students said they had cats, 13 students said they had dogs, 5 students said they had hamsters, and 10 said they did not have any of these animals as pets at home.

If there are no students that have a cat and a hamster as a pet, and there are 7 dog owners that also have a cat or a hamster, how many students only have dogs as pets?

1.9 ZIML June 2019 Division M

Below are the 20 Problems from the Division M ZIML Competition held in June 2019.
The answer key is available on p.194 in the Appendix.
Full solutions to these questions are available starting on p.166.

Problem 1
At Evan's birthday party there are 28 kids in total. Each kid is either 6 years old, 7 years old, or 8 years old.

If there were 2 fewer 8 year olds and 4 more 6 year olds, there would be the same number of 6 year olds, 7 year olds, and 8 year olds.

How many 6 year olds are there at the party?

Problem 2
Consider the following diagram, where the grid is made out of unit squares.

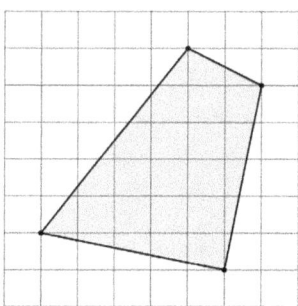

What is the area of the shaded region?

Problem 3
The university cooking club has 10 male and 20 female members. The first meeting everyone is supposed to bring their favorite cookbook. 60% of the males forget to bring their cookbook and 40% of the females forget their cookbook.

If a random member of the club is chosen, then the probability that they forgot their cookbook is $\dfrac{P}{Q}$ as a fraction in lowest terms. What is $Q - P$?

Problem 4
Larson and Manny just received their paychecks. They both received the same amount of money. Larson spent half of his money on groceries, and one third of the rest in books. Manny spent two thirds of his money paying bills, and half of the rest in groceries.

If Manny has now $600 left, how much money does Larson have left? Give your answer rounded to the nearest dollar.

Problem 5
In acute triangle $\triangle ABC$, $AB = \sqrt{41}$ and $AC = 6$. The altitude $\overline{BD}$ (with D on $\overline{AC}$) has length 5. Then $BC = \sqrt{R}$ for an integer R. What is R?

Problem 6

8 workers can finish a job in 30 hours. Assume each worker works at the same rate.

At first 4 workers work for 20 hours. Then 4 more workers come to help finish the job. How many hours will these additional workers work to finish the job? Give your answer in hours rounded to the nearest tenth.

Problem 7

What is the largest 4-digit number that leaves a remainder of 5 when divided by 8, 9, and 10?

Problem 8

Susan needs to add all the numbers from 1 to 200 using a standard calculator. How many keys will she press in total?

For example, to add 11 and 23, the following 6 key presses are needed:

$$\boxed{1}\,\boxed{1}\,\boxed{+}\,\boxed{2}\,\boxed{3}\,\boxed{=}$$

Problem 9

There is some colored candies in a bowl. It is known that the bowl contains only red, blue, and green candy, and that the ratio of the number of red, blue, and green candy is 1 : 3 : 5.

If there are 75 green candies in the bowl, how many candies are there in total?

Problem 10
Ferdinand has 3 distinct green balls, 2 distinct red balls, and 5 distinct blue balls. He wants to arrange all balls in a circle. If all balls of the same color are next to each other, in how many different ways can he arrange his balls? (Note: two circular arrangements are considered the same if one can be obtained by rotating the other.)

Problem 11
In the following diagram trapezoid $ABCD$ has area 34, $\triangle BCD$ has area 10, and $DC = 5$.

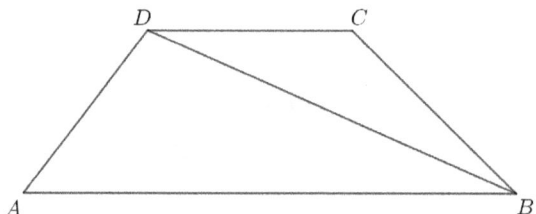

Problem 12
White, the rabbit, is standing on a staircase. When White moves, he jumps one step up with probability $\frac{2}{3}$ and one step down with probability $\frac{1}{3}$, regardless of how he moved the last time.

The probability that he comes back to the step where he started after he moves two times is $\frac{P}{Q}$ as a fraction in lowest terms. What is $Q - P$?

Problem 13
Lance is a swimming instructor during the summer. He also likes the color blue. He noticed that $\frac{2}{7}$ of his students brought a blue cap, $\frac{2}{5}$ of his students brought blue swimming trunks, and $\frac{2}{3}$ of his students brought blue goggles.

What is the least possible number of students in Lance's class?

Problem 14
In a group of 6 friends there are some who speak French, some that speak Spanish, and some that speak German. None of the friends speaks all three languages, and they all speak at least one of them. In how many different ways can this happen?

Problem 15
The diagram below shows one side of a chimney with a square base. The chimney is 10 layers tall.

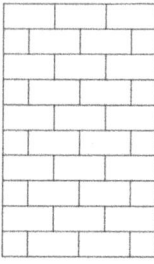

If no bricks were cut when building this chimney, how many bricks were used in total to build it?

Problem 16

What is the smallest possible value of n that would make $\dfrac{604800}{n}$ a perfect square?

Problem 17

How many possible different sums can be obtained by adding three distinct numbers from the set $\{3, 7, 11, 15, 19, 23\}$?

Problem 18

A board foot is a unit of dry volume used to measure the volume of lumber. It is the volume of a one-foot length of a board that is one foot wide and one inch thick.

At E-Wood, the price for one board foot of Cedar is $35. Ron wants to buy three pieces of Cedar, each 8 feet long, 2 feet wide, and 2 inches thick.

How much will Ron have to pay for his wood? Give your answer in dollars rounded to the nearest cent.

Problem 19

Dorothy is committed to save money to buy a video game console and some games. She decided to save $50 the first week, and each upcoming week she will save 20% more than the previous week. Her goal is to save $400. How many weeks will it take her to save at least this much money?

Problem 20
Among the numbers $1, \ldots, 30$, there are some numbers that have n factors, and there are no numbers that have more than n factors. What is n?

2. ZIML Solutions

This part of the book contains the official solutions to the problems from the nine Division M ZIML Contests from the 2018-19 School Year.

Students are encouraged to discuss and share their own methods to the problems using the Discussion Forum on ziml.areteem.org.

2.1 ZIML October 2018 Division M

Below are the solutions from the Division M ZIML Competition held in October 2018.
The problems from the contest are available on p.17.

Problem 1 Solution
Luke would finish the Evolution book in 5 days, so would have read $5 \times \frac{1}{9} = \frac{5}{9}$ of the Shakespeare book. This means he still needs to read $1 - \frac{5}{9} = \frac{4}{9}$ of the book, that is, $297 \times \frac{4}{9} = 132$ pages.

Answer: 132

Problem 2 Solution
Since the number is divisible by 33, it must be divisible by 3 and 11.

The number is divisible by 3 if and only if $a+2+a+4+a+6+a = 4a+12$ is divisible by 3. Since 12 is already divisible by 3 and $\gcd(3,4) = 1$, we need a to be a multiple of 3.

The number is divisible by 11 if and only if $a-2+a-4+a-6+a = 4a-12 = 4(a-3)$ is divisible by 11, that is, if $a-3$ is divisible by 11 (since again, $\gcd(4,11) = 1$). This only happens when $a = 3$, which is a multiple of 3, so the number 3234363 is indeed divisible by 33.

This is the only possible such number, thus the sum of all possible values of a is 3.

Answer: 3

Problem 3 Solution

If all the animals at the pet farm were monkeys there would be $2 \times 89 = 178$, that is, $282 - 178 = 104$ less legs than there actually are.

Swapping a monkey for a 4-legged animal increases leg count by $4 - 2 = 2$, so we need to swap $104 \div 2 = 52$ monkeys for either cats or dogs.

Since there are three times as many dogs as cats in the farm, there are $52 \div 4 = 13$ cats and $13 \times 3 = 39$ dogs.

Answer: 39

Problem 4 Solution

Notice the side length of the big square is three times the side length of the small squares, so we can split the rectangle in small squares like in the diagram below.

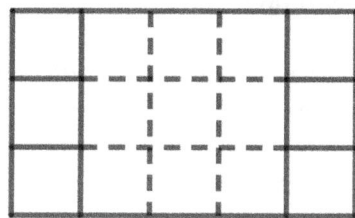

Since the area of the big square is 20 more square units than the area of 4 small squares combined, the area of 5 small squares is 20 square units, so each small square has area $20 \div 5 = 4$, and therefore has side length 2.

Thus the rectangle has dimensions $3 \times 2 = 6$ by $5 \times 5 = 10$. Hence its perimeter is $2 \times (6 + 10) = 32$.

Answer: 32

Problem 5 Solution

We are looking for the smallest possible number that leaves a remainder of 5 when divided by 9, and a remainder of 2 when divided by 8.

The first few numbers that leave a remainder of 5 when divided by 9 are $5, 14, 23, 32, 41, 50, 59, 68, \ldots$, and the remainders of these when dividing by 8 are $5, 6, 7, 0, 1, 2, 3, 4, \ldots$.

Then the smallest number that leaves a remainder of 5 when dividing by 9 and a remainder of 2 when dividing by 8 is 50. That is, the pirates collected 50 coins.

Answer: 50

Problem 6 Solution

Let's pretend Summer has indeed 23 more blue pens and 9 less black pens. Then she has $342 + 23 - 9 = 354$ pens in total, and the ratio of black pens to blue pens is $3 : 1$. This means she has $356 \div (1+3) = 89$ blue pens.

Since we assumed she had 23 more blue pens, she actually has $89 - 23 = 66$ blue pens.

Answer: 66

Problem 7 Solution

Let O be the center of the circle. Then $\triangle AOB$ is isosceles with two sides of length 6 and one angle of $120°$. Note this triangle has the same area as an equilateral triangle with side length 6, that is, area

$$\frac{\sqrt{3}}{4} \times 6^2 = 9\sqrt{3}.$$

The top portion of the shaded region is what is left after removing from a sector of $180°$ $\triangle AOB$ and two sectors that have combined area equal to that of a sector of $60°$. The bottom portion of the shaded region is a sector of $180°$.

Altogether the shaded region is equal to the area of a sector of $360° - 60° = 300°$ minus the area of $\triangle AOB$, that is

$$\frac{300}{360} \times \pi \times 6^2 - 9\sqrt{3} = 30\pi - 9\sqrt{3}.$$

Thus $A + B = 30 - 9 = 21$.

Answer: 21

Problem 8 Solution
Note $10 = 9 + 1 = (1+1) \times (4+1)$. Thus, a number that has 10 factors must be of the form p^9 with p prime, or pq^4 with p and q distinct primes.

We know the number will have $25 = 5^2$ as a factor, so the number should be 5^9 or $p \times 5^4$ for some prime p. We will obtain the smallest possible number when $p = 2$, so the number we are looking for is $2 \times 5^4 = 1250$.

Answer: 1250

Problem 9 Solution
Since Lisha can finish the job in 6 hours, and Brandee can finish the job in 4 hours, in one hour they can wash $\frac{1}{6} + \frac{1}{4} = \frac{5}{12}$ of the dishes.

After Lisha works for 2 hours, there are still $1 - \frac{2}{6} = \frac{2}{3}$ of the dishes left to wash.

Washing together $\frac{2}{3}$ of the dishes will take them $\frac{2}{3} \div \frac{5}{12} = \frac{8}{5} = 1.6$ hours. So, Lisha washed dishes for $2 + 1.6 = 3.6$ hours.

Answer: 3.6

Problem 10 Solution

There are $\binom{10}{2} = 45$ ways to choose 2 cards.

In the stack of cards there are 5 even and 5 odd numbers. To have an even product it is enough to have at least one of the two numbers to be even. There are $\binom{5}{2} = 10$ ways to choose two odd numbers. Thus, the probability that he chooses at least one even number is $1 - \dfrac{10}{45} = \dfrac{7}{9} = 0.\overline{7} \approx 77.8\%$

Answer: 77.8

Problem 11 Solution

Since $GF = \dfrac{1}{3}DC$, the area of $\triangle EGF$ is $\dfrac{1}{6}$ of the area of $ABCD$, that is, $60 \div 6 = 10$. Since I, H are the midpoints of their respective sides, K and J are too.

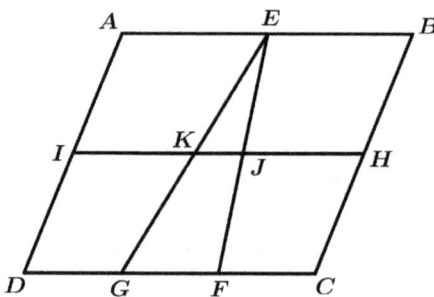

Thus, $\triangle EKJ \sim \triangle EGF$, the ratio of their sides is $1 : 2$, and the ratio of their areas is then $1 : 4$. Therefore area of $\triangle EKJ$ is $10 \div 4 = 2.5$.

Answer: 2.5

2.1 ZIML October 2018 Division M

Problem 12 Solution
Since $\text{lcm}(a,b,c) = 2^3 \times 3 \times 5^2$ and $\text{lcm}(a,b) = 2^3 \times 5$, 3 and 5^2 must be factors of c, and since $\gcd(a,b,c) = 2 \times 5$, 2 must be a factor of c as well.

Thus, the smallest possible value of c that fits in this scenario is $c = 2 \times 3 \times 5^2 = 150$.

Answer: 150

Problem 13 Solution
Note the order in which she buys the car fresheners is not important, so we can use stars and bars, with 6 stars and $5 - 1 = 4$ bars, to find how many ways she can buy them. That is, Caprice can buy he car air fresheners in $\binom{6+5-1}{5-1} = 210$ different ways.

Answer: 210

Problem 14 Solution
At Linguine's they can serve an average of $24 \times 4 = 96$ customers per hour. At Tacos Don Julio they can serve an average of $52 \times 6 = 312$ customers per hour. Thus the ratio of hungry customers that went to Linguine's to the number of hungry customers that went to Tacos Don Julio is $96 : 312 = 4 : 13$.

So, there were $153 \times \dfrac{13}{17} = 117$ hungry customers at Tacos Don Julio.

Answer: 117

Problem 15 Solution

There are $\binom{15}{2} = 105$ different ways he can grab 2 candies out of the bag.

There are $\binom{7}{2} = 21$ ways both of them are chocolates, $\binom{4}{2} = 6$ ways both of them are gummies, and $\binom{4}{2} = 6$ ways both of them are packs of gum. Thus, there are $21 + 6 + 6 = 33$ ways he could grab two of the same kind of candy.

Therefore, the probability that he grabs two different kind of candy is $1 - \dfrac{33}{105} = \dfrac{24}{35}$. Thus $Q - P = 11$.

Answer: 11

Problem 16 Solution

Since we don't want any bears sitting next to each other, we can start by arranging the Barbie's in a circle and then sitting the bears between Barbie's (at most one bear between two consecutive Barbie's). Since the Barbie's are sitting in a circle, there are $\dfrac{7!}{7} = 720$ ways of sitting them, and this creates 7 spaces between them for the bears to sit. Thus, there are $7 \times 6 \times 5 \times 4 = 840$ different ways to pick the 4 seats for the bears.

Altogether the bears and Barbie's can seat around the table in $720 \times 840 = 604800$ different ways.

Answer: 604800

Problem 17 Solution

Since all polygons in the diagram are regular, $\angle MAB = 60° + 90° + 108° + 120° - 360° = 18°$. Thus, $\angle AMB = 180° - 60° - 18° = 102°$.

Answer: 102

Problem 18 Solution

We can split the rhombus into 4 congruent right triangles, and rearrange the figure to form a rectangle like in the diagram below.

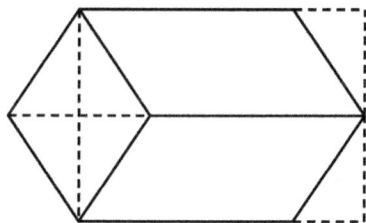

Since each side of the rhombus has length 10 and the larger diagonal of the rhombus has length 16, each small right triangle has hypotenuse 10, and legs $16 \div 2 = 8$ and 6 ($(6, 8, 10)$ is a Pythagorean triple).

Thus, the rectangle has length $17 + 6 = 23$ and width 16. Therefore the area of the figure is $23 \times 16 = 368$.

Answer: 368

Problem 19 Solution

Since we are only interested in the remainder when we divide by 7, we can work with the numbers (mod 7).

$2018 \equiv 2 \pmod{7}$, thus the sum has the same remainder as $2^{2018} + 3^{2019}$. Note the remainders (mod 7) of powers of 2 follow a pattern $2, 4, 1, 2, 4, 1 \ldots$, and the powers of 3 follow a pattern $3, 2, 6, 4, 5, 1, 3, 2, \ldots$.

Since the powers of 2 follow a pattern that repeats every 3 numbers and $2018 \equiv 2 \pmod 3$, $2^{2018} \equiv 4 \pmod 7$. Since the powers of 3 follow a pattern that repeats every 6 numbers and $2019 \equiv 3 \pmod 6$, $3^{2019} \equiv 6 \pmod 7$. That is, $2018^{2018} \times 2019^{2019} \equiv 4 \times 6 \equiv 24 \equiv 3$. Thus the remainder after dividing by 7 is 3.

Answer: 3

Problem 20 Solution

Since the video game can arrive any time between $7:00$ AM and $11:00$ AM, and Jeff's car pool buddy can arrive any time between $8:00$ AM and $9:00$ AM, we can graph the possible (package, carpool) arrival times in a rectangle. For example, the point $(7.5, 8.5)$ means the package arrives at $7:30$ and Jeff's carpool buddy arrives at $8:30$.

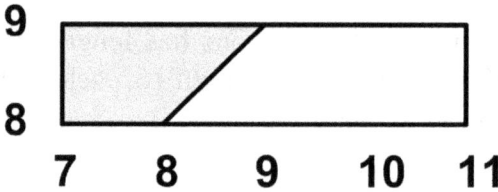

The times where the package arrives before Jeff leaves for work are represented by the shaded region.

The whole arrival times rectangle has an area of $1 \times 4 = 4$ units and the shaded region has an area of $(1 + 2) \times 1 \div 2 = 1.5$ units.

So, the probability that the video game arrives before Jeff leaves for work is $\dfrac{1.5}{4} = \dfrac{3}{8}$. Thus, $Q - P = 5$.

Answer: 5

2.2 ZIML November 2018 Division M

Below are the solutions from the Division M ZIML Competition held in November 2018.
The problems from the contest are available on p.25.

Problem 1 Solution
The shaded region is equal to the area of both squares combined minus a triangle with base $3+5=8$ and height 3, and a triangle with base 5 and height 5.

Thus, the shaded region has area
$$3^2 + 5^2 - (8 \times 3 \div 2 + 5 \times 5 \div 2) = 9.5.$$

Answer: 9.5

Problem 2 Solution
Since the group of 30 ants has $30 \div 5 = 6$ times as many ants as a group that can finish the job in 12 hours, they can finish the job in $12 \div 6 = 2$ hours.

Answer: 2

Problem 3 Solution
We can represent the arrival times of Albert, Bertha and Carl with a cube of side length 1, and thus, volume 1.

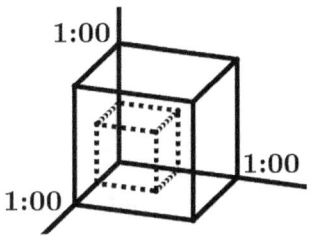

The region of the cube that represents the times where all three of them arrive before 12:30, is a cube with side length $\frac{1}{2}$.

Therefore, the probability that the arrive in time to order the super special lunch menu is $\left(\frac{1}{2}\right)^2 = \frac{1}{8}$. Thus, $Q - P = 8 - 1 = 7$.

Answer: 7

Problem 4 Solution
Note $72 = 2^3 \times 3^2$ and $43200 = 2^6 \times 3^3 \times 5^2$. To make b as large as possible, we want a as small as possible.

Since a is a perfect square, its smallest possible value is $2^6 \times 3^2 = 576$, and since $a \times b = 72 \times 43200$, the largest possible value of b is $2^3 \times 3^3 \times 5^2 = 5400$.

Answer: 5400

Problem 5 Solution
The sum of the first 13 assignments that Mr. Rivers graded is $13 \times 82 = 1066$ points.

With the two new assignments raising the average grade to 83 points, the sum of all assignments is $15 \times 83 = 1245$ points.

This means the grades of the two late submissions add up to $1245 - 1066 = 179$, and since they are 7 points apart, the one with the lower score was $(179 - 7) \div 2 = 86$ points.

Answer: 86

Problem 6 Solution
Factoring 66 and 78 we have

$$66 = 2 \times 3 \times 11 \text{ and } 78 = 2 \times 3 \times 13.$$

2.2 ZIML November 2018 Division M

As the number is multiple of both 66 and 78, it must be a multiple of
$$\text{lcm}(66, 78) = 2 \times 3 \times 11 \times 13 = 858.$$
Since $10000 \div 858 = 11$ with remainder 562, the largest multiple of 858 with 4 digits is $11 \times 858 = 9438$, which has all different digits.

Clearly 858×10 has 3 different digits, so we try $858 \times 9 = 7722$ which has exactly two different digits, so it is the number we are looking for.

Answer: 7722

Problem 7 Solution
Since AFJ is an isosceles triangle with $AF = AJ$ and $\angle FAJ = 20°$,
$$\angle AFJ = \angle AJF = (180° - 20°) \div 2 = 80°.$$

Using vertical angles and the fact that $\triangle BGF$, and $\triangle CHG$ are both isosceles, $\triangle AFJ$, $\triangle BGF$, and $\triangle CHG$, all have angles of $20°, 80°, 80°$. Hence,
$$\angle BHE = 180° - \angle EHD = 180° - 80° = 100°.$$

Answer: 100

Problem 8 Solution
Larry does
$$24, 29, 34, 39, \ldots$$
sit ups each day. These numbers form an arithmetic sequence. October 31st is 30 days after October 1st, so he does $24 + 30 \times 5 = 174$ sit ups the last day.

Adding up this arithmetic sequence, Larry does

$$\frac{24 + 174}{2} \times 31 = 99 \times 31 = 3069$$

sit ups in total.

Answer: 3069

Problem 9 Solution

3 workers can build 5 dining tables in 1 week, so 3 workers can build $5 \times 2 = 10$ tables in 2 weeks.

Since the goal is to make 50 dining tables, Mr. Furn E. Ture would need $50 \div 10 = 5$ groups of 3 workers, that is $5 \times 3 = 15$ workers in total.

This means Mr. Furn E. Ture needs to hire an additional $15 - 3 = 12$ workers to be able to finish on time.

Answer: 12

Problem 10 Solution

Let n be the number we are looking for. Note then $n + 1$ is a multiple of both, 5 and 6, and thus, is a multiple of 30.

Since $10000 \div 30 = 333$ with remainder 10, the largest possible multiple of 30 with 4 digits is $333 \times 30 = 9990$.

Therefore $9990 - 1 = 9989$ is the largest 4-digit number that leaves remainder 4 when divided by 5 and remainder 5 when divided by 6.

Answer: 9989

Problem 11 Solution

If all the packs of crayons she bought had 10 crayons, she would have had in total $10 \times 13 = 130$ crayons, that is $160 - 130 = 30$

less crayons than she actually bought.

Since each pack of 15 crayons has $15 - 10 = 5$ more crayons than a pack of 10 crayons, she must have bought $30 \div 5 = 6$ packs of 15 crayons and $13 - 6 = 7$ packs of 10 crayons.

Thus, she spent a total of $7 \times 2.50 + 6 \times 3.50 = 38.50$ dollars.

Answer: 38.5

Problem 12 Solution
Since the area of $ABCD$ is 15 and its bases have length 2 and 8, its height is $15 \div (2 + 8) \times 2 = 3$.

Therefore the area of $\triangle ABC$ is $\frac{1}{2} \times 2 \times 3 = 3$.

Note the ratio of the areas of $\triangle ABE$ and $\triangle BEC$ is $1 : 4$, so the area of $\triangle ABE$ is $3 \div (1 + 4) = 0.6$.

Answer: 0.6

Problem 13 Solution
Using the positive version of stars and bars there are
$$\binom{10-1}{4-1} = \binom{9}{3} = 84$$
ways for the four numbers to add up to 10.

There are $10^4 = 10000$ total ways of choosing the numbers, hence the probability is
$$\frac{84}{10000} = \frac{21}{2500}$$
so $Q - P = 2500 - 21 = 2479$.

Answer: 2479

Problem 14 Solution

Since each time she drank half of the coffee/milk mix she had, the 80%/20% coffee/milk mix she started with makes for $\frac{1}{2} \times \frac{1}{2} = \frac{1}{4}$ of the mix she has in the end.

Similarly, the half cup of coffee that she added first makes for $\frac{1}{4}$ of her final mix as well.

Therefore, the coffee in her final mix makes for

$$\frac{4}{5} \times \frac{1}{4} + \frac{1}{4} = \frac{9}{20}$$

of the cup, that is, 45% of Lizzie's cup is coffee.

Answer: 45

Problem 15 Solution

The rhombus has two angles of 120° and two angles of 60°, so the minor diagonal splits the rhombus into two equilateral triangles of side length 12.

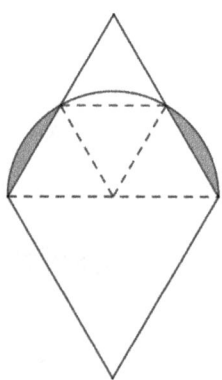

Furthermore, we can split each of these in four equilateral triangles with side length 6.

2.2 ZIML November 2018 Division M

Then each of the two portions of the shaded region is a 60° sector of a circle of radius 6 minus an equilateral triangle of side length 6.

Thus, the shaded area is equal to

$$2 \times \left(\frac{1}{6} \times 6^2 \times \pi - \frac{\sqrt{3}}{4} \times 6^2 \right) = -18\sqrt{3} + 12\pi.$$

Therefore $A + B - C = -18 + 3 - 12 = -27$.

Answer: -27

Problem 16 Solution

First note $\triangle ABC$ is a right triangle, so using Pythagorean triples we have $AC = 5$. Since $AB = AE = 3$ are both radii, we know $CE = 5 + 3 = 8$.

$\triangle EDC$ and $\triangle ABC$ are both right triangles that share $\angle C$. Hence they are similar, with ratio of sides $8 : 5$. Thus

$$CD = 4 \times \frac{8}{5} = \frac{32}{5} \text{ and } ED = 3 \times \frac{8}{5} = \frac{24}{5}.$$

Hence the area of $\triangle EDC$ is

$$\frac{1}{2} \times \frac{32}{5} \times \frac{24}{5} = \frac{384}{25}.$$

Thus $P + Q = 384 + 25 = 409$.

Answer: 409

Problem 17 Solution

Arrange first all white pieces in a circle. There are $6 + 2 + 2 = 10$ white pieces, so there are $\frac{10!}{10} = 9!$ ways of arranging them in a

circle. Since pieces of the same kind are identical, there are
$$\frac{9!}{6! \times 2! \times 2!} = 126$$
ways to arrange the white pieces in a circle.

This creates 10 spaces for the black pieces to be in. We need to choose 2 of these 10 spaces for the black pieces, which can be done in $10 \times 9 = 90$ ways.

Therefore, there are $126 \times 90 = 11340$ ways to arrange all chess pieces in a circle.

Answer: 11340

Problem 18 Solution
Let's pretend that Tiffani has 4 more super hero stamps. Then she has $209 + 4 = 213$ stamps in total, and she has three times as many super hero stamps as space stamps, and she has $4 + 7 = 11$ more super hero stamps than Cinderella stamps.

Let's pretend then also that she has 11 more Cinderella stamps, for a total of $213 + 11 = 224$ stamps, having now the same number of super hero stamps and Cinderella stamps.

This means she has $314 \div (3 + 1 + 3) = 32$ space stamps, $32 \times 3 - 4 = 92$ super hero stamps, and $92 - 7 = 85$ Cinderella stamps.

Answer: 85

Problem 19 Solution
Since $1400 = 2^3 \times 5^2 \times 7$, Primrose gave away $(3+1) \times (2+1) \times (1+1) = 24$ numbers in total.

The only odd numbers are factors of $5^2 \times 7$, so there are $(2+1)(1+1) = 6$ odd numbers, and hence werewolves, in total. The remaining $24 - 6 = 18$ are ghosts.

All werewolves had odd numbers, so in the first round of the contest they were all paired with a ghost, and thus, they all lost.

Therefore $24 \div 2 = 12$ ghosts advanced to the second round of the costume contest.

Answer: 12

Problem 20 Solution

Note all even numbers are raised to powers that are at least 2, so they are all multiples of 4.

Hence the sum will have the same remainder as that of the sum $1 + 3^3 + 5^5 + \cdots + 21^{21}$ when divided by 4.

Even powers of odd numbers all have remainder 1 when divided by 4, so this last sum has the same remainder as $1 + 3 + 5 + \cdots + 21 = 11^2 = 121$, when divided by 4, that is, the remainder is 1.

Answer: 1

2.3 ZIML December 2018 Division M

Below are the solutions from the Division M ZIML Competition held in December 2018.
The problems from the contest are available on p.35.

Problem 1 Solution
If $\star = \times$ we have a geometric sequence
$$3, 3 \times 2, 3 \times 2^2, 3 \times 2^3, \ldots.$$
In this case, the tenth term is $3 \times 2^9 = 3 \times 512 = 1536$, so $G = 1536$.

If $\star = +$ we have an arithmetic sequence
$$3, 3+2, 3+2 \times 2, 3+2 \times 3, \ldots.$$
In this case, the tenth term is $3 + 2 \times 9 = 21$, so $A = 21$.

Therefore $G - A = 1536 - 21 = 1515$.

Answer: 1515

Problem 2 Solution
The cubes have volume $1 = 1^3$, $8 = 2^3$, $27 = 3^3$, and $64 = 4^3$ so they have side lengths of 1, 2, 3, and 4. Therefore they separately have surface areas of
$$6 \times 1^2 = 6, 6 \times 2^2 = 24, 6 \times 3^2 = 54, \text{ and } 6 \times 4^2 = 96.$$
However, with the pieces glued together we need to remove some area. Where the cubes of side lengths 3 and 4 are stacked, their overlap is the bottom of the cube with side length 3. We need to remove this from the calculated surface area of both cubes. Thus we need to subtract $2 \times 3^2 = 18$.

2.3 ZIML December 2018 Division M

Similarly we must remove $2 \times 2^2 = 8$ (for where the cubes of side length 2 and 3 are glued together) and $2 \times 1^2 = 2$ (for where the cubes of side length 1 and 2 are glued together). This gives a surface area of

$$6 + 24 + 54 + 96 - 18 - 8 - 2 = 152,$$

as our final answer.

Answer: 152

Problem 3 Solution

The remainder when any number is divided by 9 is equal to the remainder of the sum of the number's digits divided by 9. The sum of the digits is

$$3 + 7 + 3 + 7 + \cdots + 3 = 3 \times 19 + 7 \times 18.$$

Note automatically 7×18 is a multiple of 9, so we can ignore it. The remainder when $3 \times 19 = 57$ is divided by 9 is 3, so our final remainder is 3.

Answer: 3

Problem 4 Solution

Pat spends 0.5 hours walking to school and 0.75 hours walking back, so his total time spent traveling is 1.25 hours.

Since his average speed for the round trip is 3.5 miles per hour, he travels $1.25 \times 3.5 = 4.375$ miles. This means the distance from his house to the school is $4.375 \div 2 \approx 2.2$ miles.

Answer: 2.2

Problem 5 Solution

Note all denominators are powers of 2, so a fraction will be irreducible if and only if the numerator is an odd number. The numerators are consecutive numbers from 1 to 10, so exactly half of them have an odd number.

This means 5 of the fractions are irreducible.

Answer: 5

Problem 6 Solution

Consider the labeling below

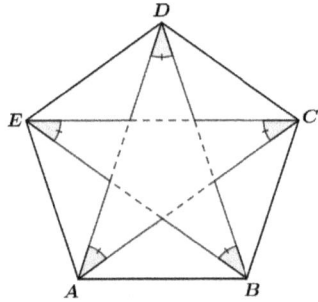

We know the pentagon is regular so all the angles and sides are equal. All the interior angles are therefore

$$\frac{180° \times (5-2)}{5} = 180° \times \frac{3}{5} = 108°.$$

All the sides are equal, so $\triangle ABC$ is isosceles. Therefore

$$\angle BAC = \angle BCA = \frac{180° - 108°}{2} = 36°.$$

Identical reasoning gives $\angle EAD = \angle EDA = 36°$. Therefore the marked angle near A is equal to

$$\angle BAE - \angle BAC - \angle EAD = 108° - 36° - 36° = 36°.$$

Therefore $K = 36$.

Answer: 36

2.3 ZIML December 2018 Division M

Problem 7 Solution

According to the pie chart, 25% of the students chose Strawberry as their favorite flavor. Thus, there are $20 \div 0.25 = 80$ students in total.

Of those, 55% chose chocolate as their favorite flavor, that is, $80 \times 0.55 = 44$ students.

Answer: 44

Problem 8 Solution

Clearly the mode is 7, which occurs 6 times.

There are
$$2+1+3+6+4+3+2 = 21$$
total numbers, so the median is the 11th number. This is also 7.

Adding up all 21 numbers we have
$$2 \times 2 + 4 \times 1 + 6 \times 3 + 7 \times 6 + 8 \times 4 + 9 \times 3 + 10 \times 2$$
$$= 4 + 4 + 18 + 42 + 32 + 27 + 20$$
$$= 147$$

Thus the mean is $147 \div 21 = 7$.

Hence the mean, median, and mode are all 7, with sum 21.

Answer: 21

Problem 9 Solution

In one minute, one big bird would drink $\dfrac{1}{30}$ of the water and one small bird would drink $\dfrac{1}{50}$ of the water. So, in one minute, 2 big birds and 1 small bird can drink
$$2 \times \frac{1}{25} + \frac{1}{50} = \frac{5}{50} = \frac{1}{10}$$

of the water in the fountain.

Therefore, the three birds would take 10 minutes to drink all the water in the bird fountain.

Answer: 10

Problem 10 Solution
If we line up the 5 players first, there are

$$5! = 5 \times 4 \times 3 \times 2 \times 1 = 120$$

total ways.

Coach Greg does not stand on the ends, so he is in one of the four spots in the middle. Hence there are $120 \times 4 = 480$ total photos.

Answer: 480

Problem 11 Solution
Note $120 = 3 \times 4 \times 10$, so the number must be a multiple of 3, 4 and 10.

Since it is a multiple of 10 it must end in 0, and since it is a multiple of 4, the last two digits must be multiples of 4. So, the last two digits could be 00, 20, 40, 60, or 80.

A number is a multiple of 3 if and only if the sum of its digits is a multiple of 3. Since $2+0+1+8 = 11$, the last two digits should add up to a number that is 1 more than a multiple of 3. Out of the possible choices, the only one that works is 40.

Hence, the number is 201840

Answer: 201840

2.3 ZIML December 2018 Division M

Problem 12 Solution
Since $AD = 24$, and $AB : BC : CD = 3 : 4 : 1 = 9 : 12 : 3$, the semicircles have diameter 3, 9, 12 and 24.

Altogether, the lengths of the semicircles add up to

$$\frac{1}{2} \times (3+9+12+24) \times \pi = 24\pi.$$

Note the actual lengths of the small semicircles do not matter as long as they add up to 24, so the lengths of all semicircles add up to the length of a circumference of diameter 24.

Answer: 24

Problem 13 Solution
There are 6^3 total outcomes.

It is possible to list all the outcomes $(1+1+3, 1+2+2,$ etc.) that sum to 5. Otherwise using the positive version of stars and bars there are $\binom{5-1}{2} = \binom{4}{2} = 6$ ways the three rolls can sum to 6.

Therefore the probability is

$$\frac{6}{6^3} = \frac{1}{6^2} = \frac{1}{36}$$

so $P + Q = 1 + 36 = 37$.

Answer: 37

Problem 14 Solution
If Paul had carried 2 packs less, they would have carried $50 - 2 = 48$ packs in total, and Paul would have carried exactly three times as many as Mary.

This means Mary carried $48 \div (3+1) = 12$ packs, and Paul carried $50 - 12 = 38$ packs.

Answer: 12

Problem 15 Solution
Since there are the same number of rhombi on each edge of the parallelogram, it is actually a rhombus with side length $40 \div 4 = 10$, and so there are 10 rhombi per side.

Thus, in total there are $10 \times 10 = 100$ rhombi.

Answer: 100

Problem 16 Solution
Note every hour, the alert is off by 5 extra minutes. The next time the alert will be correct for 8:00 AM is when the alert is off by an entire day. Since 1 day is

$$1 \times 24 \times 60 = 1440$$

minutes, it will take

$$1440 \div 5 = 288$$

hours until the alert is correct again.

Answer: 288

Problem 17 Solution
If all decks had the 2 extra cards, Phil would have $85 \times 54 = 4590$ cards in total.

That is $4590 - 4480 = 110$ more cards than he actually has. This means he had $110 \div 2 = 55$ standard decks.

Answer: 55

2.3 ZIML December 2018 Division M

Problem 18 Solution

For the number N to have exactly 16 factors, with at least 3 prime factors, it must be of the form $N = p^2 \times q \times r$ or $N = p \times q \times r \times s$ for distinct prime numbers p, q, r, s.

Using the smallest possible prime numbers will yield the smallest possible values of N. We have then $2^2 \times 3 \times 5 = 120$ is the smallest possible value of N.

Answer: 120

Problem 19 Solution

Adding up all the edges (made of toothpicks) we know Monty used
$$3+4+5+6+8 = 26$$
toothpicks in total. As an octagon has 8 sides, the probability that the first toothpick he picks was from the octagon is $\dfrac{8}{26}$. Similarly, the probability the second toothpick was from the pentagon is $\dfrac{5}{25}$. This gives a probability of
$$\frac{8}{26} \times \frac{5}{25} = \frac{4}{13 \times 5} = \frac{4}{65}.$$
Therefore $S - R = 65 - 4 = 61$.

Answer: 61

Problem 20 Solution

Let DJ and DK be altitudes of $ABCD$ and $DEFA$, respectively, perpendicular to AD.

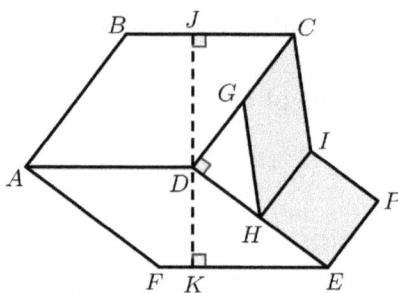

Since the area of $ABCD$ is 20, and the area of $DEFA$ is 15, we have that $DJ = 20 \div 5 = 4$ and $DK = 15 \div 5 = 3$.

Then DCJ and EDK are congruent $3-4-5$ triangles, and so $\angle EDC = 90°$.

Therefore $EHIP$ is a square with side length $5 \div 2 = 2.5$, and $CIHG$ is a parallelogram with base 2.5 and height 2.5. Hence, the shaded area is $5 \times 2.5 = 12.5$.

Answer: 12.5

2.4 ZIML January 2019 Division M

Below are the solutions from the Division M ZIML Competition held in January 2019.
The problems from the contest are available on p.43.

Problem 1 Solution
Clearly all numbers from 100 to 199 are divisible by their hundreds digit.

Exactly half of the numbers between 200 and 299 are even, so there are 50 numbers that start with 2 that are divisible by their hundreds digit.

Since $299 \div 3$ is 99 with remainder 2 and $399 \div 3 = 133$, there are $133 - 99 = 34$ multiples of 3 between 300 and 399.

Lastly, 400 is divisible by 4, so there are in total $100 + 50 + 34 + 1 = 185$ numbers between 100 and 400 that are divisible by their hundreds digit.

Answer: 185

Problem 2 Solution
The Cookie Emporium received 80 boxes of Super Duper Chocolate cookies, which represent 20% of the total number of boxes shipped to stores, so they shipped $80 \div 0.2 = 400$ boxes of Super Duper Chocolate cookies. Similarly, we can see they shipped $150 \div 0.5 = 300$ boxes of Coco-coffee cookies, and $240 \div 0.3 = 800$ boxes of Sparkling Sugar cookies.

Therefore, The Great Cookie Factory shipped $400 + 300 + 800 = 1500$ boxes of cookies this month.

Answer: 1500

Problem 3 Solution

Draw perpendicular lines through the midpoints of the sides of the triangles. Extending the bases of the trapezoid this forms a rectangle as in the diagram below.

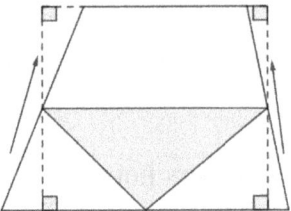

By rearranging the triangles as shown, we see that the trapezoid has the same area as a rectangle. The shaded triangle has the same base as the rectangle, but half the height. Therefore the area of the rectangle (and hence the trapezoid) is four times the area of the triangle. Our answer is thus $4 \times 17 = 68$.

Answer: 68

Problem 4 Solution

Start by arranging the blue and green cards in a line. Since all cards of the same color are identical, we just need to choose which of the $3 + 4 = 7$ spots in line will be taken by blue cards. This can be done in $\binom{7}{3} = 35$ ways.

Now place red cards in the spaces created in between the other cards. There are 8 spaces created by the cards, and we need to pick 5 of them, so this can be done in $\binom{8}{5} = 56$ ways.

Thus, altogether the cards can be arranged in $35 \times 56 = 1960$

different ways.

Answer: 1960

Problem 5 Solution

Consider first $\triangle ABC$. Since the octagon is regular we know $AB = BC$ and $\angle ABC = 135°$. Therefore

$$\angle BAC = \angle BCA = \frac{180° - 135°}{2} = 22.5°.$$

Combining with $\angle BCD = 135°$ we thus have

$$\angle ACD = \angle BCD - \angle BCA = 135° - 22.5° = 112.5°.$$

Therefore $\angle JCD = 180° - 112.5° = 67.5°$. As identical reasoning gives $\angle JDC = 67.5°$, we have

$$\begin{aligned}\angle AJF &= \angle CJD \\ &= 180° - \angle JCD - \angle JDC \\ &= 180° - 67.5° - 67.5° \\ &= 45°\end{aligned}$$

and our answer is 45.

Answer: 45

Problem 6 Solution

In one hour Alex can finish $\frac{1}{16}$ of the job, Brittany can finish $\frac{1}{32}$ of the job, and Celeste can finish $\frac{1}{32}$ of the job.

Thus, working together for 1 hour, Alex and Celeste can finish $\frac{1}{16} + \frac{1}{32} = \frac{3}{32}$ of the job. Hence, after working together for 8 hours they finish $\frac{3}{32} \times 8 = \frac{3}{4}$ of the job. This means there is only $1 - \frac{3}{4} = \frac{1}{4}$ of the job left to do.

When the three of them work together for one hour, they can complete $\frac{1}{16} + \frac{1}{32} + \frac{1}{32} = \frac{1}{8}$ of the job. So, to finish the remaining $\frac{1}{4}$ of the job, they would need to work together for $\frac{1}{4} \div \frac{1}{8} = 2$ hours.

Therefore, Brittany worked for 2 hours.

Answer: 2

Problem 7 Solution
The shaded region is equal to the area of a trapezoid with bases 2 and 6 and height 8, minus the area of a triangle with base and height 6 and a triangle with base and height 2.

Thus, the shaded area is equal to

$$\frac{(2+6) \times 8}{2} - \frac{6 \times 6}{2} - \frac{2 \times 2}{2} = 12.$$

Answer: 12

Problem 8 Solution
In total there are 9 letters, three T's, three O's, two L's, and one F. There are 9! total rearrangements of the letters, but we need to divide by $3! \times 3! \times 2!$ for the repeated letters (as their rearrangements do not matter).

This gives an answer of

$$\frac{9!}{3! \times 3! \times 2!} = \frac{9 \times 8 \times 7!}{6 \times 6 \times 2} = 7!$$

and calculating we have $7! = 5040$.

Answer: 5040

2.4 ZIML January 2019 Division M

Problem 9 Solution
Since the ratio of the boys that like dogs to the boys that like cats is $7:3$, the number of boys in Ms. Johnson's class must be a multiple of 10. Similarly, the number of girls in Ms. Johnson's class is a multiple of 9.

The ratio of boys to girls is $5:9 = 10:18$, so the least possible number of students in Ms. Johnson's class is $10 + 18 = 28$.

Answer: 28

Problem 10 Solution
$21 = (20+1) = (2+1) \times (6+1)$, so the number we are looking form must be of the form p^{20} for p prime or $p^2 q^6$ for p, q distinct prime numbers.

Since $21 = 3 \times 7$, the number must have 3 and 7 as factors, so it is equal to either $3^2 \times 7^6$ or $7^2 \times 3^6$.

Clearly $7^2 \times 3^6 = 35721$ is smaller, so that is the number we are looking for.

Answer: 35721

Problem 11 Solution
There are $7+4+1 = 12$ balls in total. Thus, there are $\binom{12}{2} = 66$ ways to pick two of them.

Of those 66 ways to pick the two balls, there are $\binom{7}{2} = 21$ ways to pick two green balls, $\binom{4}{2} = 6$ ways to pick two red balls, and 0 ways to pick two blue balls.

Therefore, the probability that both balls are the same color is

$$\frac{21+6+0}{66} = \frac{9}{22} \text{ as a reduced fraction. Thus,}$$

$$Q - P = 22 - 9 = 13.$$

Answer: 13

Problem 12 Solution

Since the second parallelogram is formed by joining the midpoints of the first parallelogram, its area will be half of the area of the first parallelogram.

Similarly, the third parallelogram will have area equal to half of the area of the second parallelogram, that is, one fourth of the area of the first parallelogram.

Since the third parallelogram has area 31, the first parallelogram must have area $4 \times 31 = 124$.

Answer: 124

Problem 13 Solution

Start by arranging the 6 adults in a circle. This can be done in $\frac{6!}{6} = 120$ different ways.

This creates 6 spaces between them where the kids can seat. The first kid has 6 spaces to choose from, the second 5, and the third has 4 choices.

Therefore, there are $120 \times 6 \times 5 \times 4 = 14400$ different ways to seat the adults and children in the table.

Answer: 14400

2.4 ZIML January 2019 Division M

Problem 14 Solution
If Rosabella had bought 23 packs of glitter inked pens, she would have bought $23 \times 2 = 46$ pens in total. That is $54 - 46 = 8$ less pens than she actually bought. Since each pack of non-glitter pens has one more pen, this means she bought 8 packs of non-glitter inked pens and $23 - 8 = 15$ packs of glitter inked pens.

Thus, she spent $15 \times 2.50 + 8 \times 1.50 = 49.50$ dollars in total.

Answer: 49.5

Problem 15 Solution
Lorraine rides her bike for a total of $6 + 4 = 10$ miles. At an average speed of 20 miles per hour, she spends $10 \div 20 = 0.5$ hours, or 30 minutes, riding her bike.

This means she spends 1 hour and 10 minutes, or $\frac{7}{6}$ of an hour on the metro. Since she rides the metro for 35 miles, the average speed of the metro is $35 \div \frac{7}{6} = 30$ miles per hour.

Answer: 30

Problem 16 Solution
Based on the rules, before anyone is "it" a second time, everyone is "it" once. Since there are 6 friends, there are $6! = 720$ ways for this to happen.

The game ends when the last person to be "it" tags another person. As they cannot tag themselves, there are 5 choices for the final person to be tagged. Hence there are $720 \times 5 = 3600$ different possible lists.

Answer: 3600

Problem 17 Solution

Patricia's circle has area 16π, so must have radius 4. William draws two congruent circles, each with the same diameter.

To get the largest circles, William's circle have diameter equal to the radius of Patricia's circle, as shown below

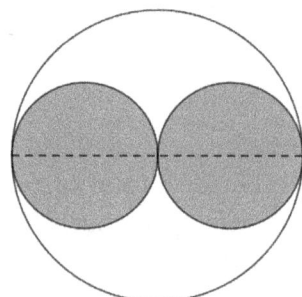

Hence William's circles each have diameter 4 and thus radius 2. Therefore William's circles cover

$$\frac{2 \times \pi(2^2)}{16\pi} = \frac{8\pi}{16\pi} = \frac{1}{2} = 50\%,$$

and $K = 50$.

Answer: 50

Problem 18 Solution

If we look at the remainders of the numbers when we divide by 4, the numbers become 1, 2, 3, 0, 1, 2, 3, 0.

Consider 5 consecutive numbers A, B, C, D, E in the list. We need both
$$A + B + C + D \text{ and } B + C + D + E$$
to have remainder 0 when we divide by 4. Hence A and E must have the same remainder when dividing by 4. Hence (still looking

at the remainders when we divide by 4) our list must be

$$A, B, C, D, A, B, C, D.$$

(For example, A could stand for both 8 and 4.) However, $1 + 2 + 3 + 0 = 6$ is not divisible by 4 so this is impossible. Therefore the answer is 0.

Answer: 0

Problem 19 Solution
The largest 5-digit number that we can make starting with 7 is 79999. Note this number has a remainder of 7 when divided by 9, so the number we are looking for is $79999 - 4 = 79992$.

Answer: 79992

Problem 20 Solution
Note that $10^n \equiv 1 \pmod{11}$ when n is even, and $10^n \equiv -1 \pmod{11}$ when n is odd. Thus, mod 11, the sum turns into

$$1^1 + (-1)^{10} + 1^{100} + (-1)^{1000} + 1^{10000} + (-1)^{100000}.$$

Therefore, the remainder of the sum after dividing by 11 is $1 + 1 + 1 + 1 + 1 + 1 = 6$.

Answer: 5

2.5 ZIML February 2019 Division M

Below are the solutions from the Division M ZIML Competition held in February 2019.
The problems from the contest are available on p.51.

Problem 1 Solution
To build one house a team of 5 workers would need to work for $2 \times 6 \times 8 = 96$ hours each. This means, building one house requires $5 \times 96 = 480$ work-hours.

To build 4 houses the team would require to $480 \times 4 = 1920$ work-hours, so each person on the team would need to work for $1920 \div 20 = 96$ hours.

Answer: 96

Problem 2 Solution
The smaller squares have area 4, so side length 2. These means the top left square has a side length of 6, each of the squares in the middle have side lengths of 4, and the square on the right has a side length of 8.

The full rectangle therefore has dimensions 18 by 8 and hence area $18 \times 8 = 144$. We find the area of the shaded region by subtracting off the unshaded portions.

The top region is a triangle with base 18 and height 4, hence area $\frac{1}{2} \times 18 \times 4 = 36$. The region on the bottom left is a triangle with base and height 8, so area $\frac{1}{2} \times 8^2 = 32$. The bottom right region is two triangles and three squares, with a combined area of

$$\frac{1}{2} \times 6^2 + \frac{1}{2} \times 4 \times 2 + 3 \times 2^2$$
$$= 18 + 4 + 12 = 34.$$

Hence the shaded region has an area of

$$144 - 36 - 32 - 34 = 42,$$

which is the answer.

Answer: 42

Problem 3 Solution

If the reading in the dashboard is accurate, David should have $168 \div 24 = 7$ gallons of gas left in the tank.

Thus, to take the tank to be $\frac{3}{4}$ full, David needs to buy $7 \div 2 = 3.5$ gallons of gas.

Answer: 3.5

Problem 4 Solution

Label the missing digits A and B so the number is $\overline{1A3B}$. Since $36 = 4 \times 9$ we need the number to be divisible by both 4 and 9.

To be divisible by 4, the last two digits, $\overline{3B}$ must be divisible by 4. Hence $B = 2$ or $B = 6$.

To be divisible by 9, the sum of the digits $1 + A + 3 + B = 4 + A + B$ must be divisible by 9.

If $B = 2$, then $6 + A$ is divisible by 9, so $A = 3$. This gives the number 1332. If $B = 6$, then $10 + A$ is divisible by 9, so $A = 8$. This gives the larger number 1836, the answer.

Answer: 1836

Problem 5 Solution

If the number is N, then $N + 5$ is divisible by 12, 16, and 21. Therefore $N + 5 = \text{lcm}(12, 16, 21)$.

$12 = 2^2 \times 3$, $16 = 2^4$, and $21 = 3 \times 7$, so
$$\text{lcm}(12, 16, 21) = 2^4 \times 3 \times 7 = 336.$$
Hence the smallest number is $336 - 5 = 331$.

Answer: 331

Problem 6 Solution

If all the dishes were "not too spicy" Isiah would use $2 \times 12 = 24$ chilies in total.

He actually used $45 - 24 = 21$ more chilies. Since every "spicy" dish uses $5 - 2 = 3$ extra chilies, Isiah must have cooked $21 \div 3 = 7$ "spicy" dishes for the potluck.

Answer: 7

Problem 7 Solution

Using 3-4-5 triangles, we see the three quarter circles have radii 3, 4 and 5, as shown below.

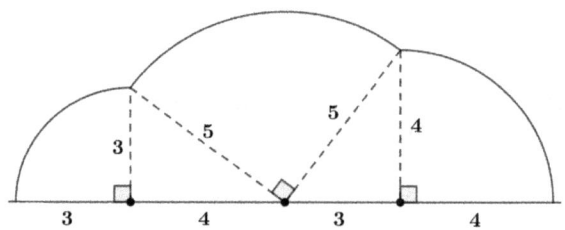

Therefore the length of the curve is
$$\frac{1}{4}(2\pi \times 3) + \frac{1}{4}(2\pi \times 5) + \frac{1}{4}(2\pi \times 4)$$
$$= \frac{3}{2}\pi + \frac{5}{2}\pi + 2\pi$$
$$= 6\pi.$$

2.5 ZIML February 2019 Division M

Hence $P \times Q = 6 \times 1 = 6$.

Answer: 6

Problem 8 Solution

We consider the different possible sums. The smallest possible sum is
$$2+2+2+2+2 = 10.$$
The largest possible sum is
$$10+10+10+10+10 = 50.$$
All the sums of 10, 12, 14, up to 50 are possible, a total of
$$(50-10) \div 2 + 1 = 21$$
different sums. Each of these sums leads to a different average, thus there are 21 different averages.

Answer: 21

Problem 9 Solution

Since $100 \div 3 = 33$ with remainder 1, there are 33 numbers divisible by 3 from 1 to 100. Similarly there are $100 \div 5 = 20$ numbers divisible by 5 and 9 divisible by 11 (as $100 \div 11 = 9$ with remainder 1).

However, all the multiples of $3 \times 5 = 15$ are divisible by both 3 and 5, all multiples of $3 \times 11 = 33$ are divisible by 3 and 11, and all multiples of $5 \times 11 = 55$ are divisible by 5 and 11. (No numbers are divisible by all 3.)

Identical reasoning to the above gives 6 multiples of 15, 3 multiples of 33 and 1 multiple of 55 that we need to remove. These are each counted twice (for example, 15 as a multiple of 3 and again as a multiple of 5). Hence there are
$$33 + 20 + 9 - 2 \times 6 - 2 \times 3 - 2 \times 1 = 42$$

integers divisible by exactly one of 3, 5, and 11 from 1 to 100.

Answer: 52

Problem 10 Solution
Factoring we have
$$22^{30} \times 26^{23} = 2^{30} \times 11^{30} \times 2^{23} \times 13^{23}$$
$$= 2^{53} \times 11^{30} \times 13^{23}.$$

To be a perfect cube, factors must have each exponent a multiple of 3. For the exponent of 2 this means
$$0, 3, 6, \ldots, 51$$
are possible, a total of $51 \div 3 + 1 = 17 + 1 = 18$ options.

Similarly there are $30 \div 3 + 1 = 11$ options for the exponent of 11 and $21 \div 3 + 1 = 8$ options for the exponent of 13. This gives a total of
$$18 \times 11 \times 8 = 1584$$
factors that are perfect cubes.

Answer: 1584

Problem 11 Solution
The riders will each drive their own car, so they just need to decide how many of the passengers will be in each car. This is equivalent to placing $8 - 3 = 5$ identical balls in 3 distinct boxes. Using stars and bars we have there are $\binom{5+3-1}{3-1} = 21$ different ways. Note however, this includes the cases where 5 passengers ride on the same car, which can't happen since a car fits up to 5 people. This means 3 of the options we counted before are not

possible (one for each car), so there are in total $21 - 3 = 18$ ways to decide how many passengers will ride in each car.

Answer: 18

Problem 12 Solution

Let $[ABCD]$ denote the area of $ABCD$ and J denote the midpoint of CD. Since E and I are midpoints of their respective sides,

$$[AEI] = \frac{1}{2} \times \frac{1}{2} \times \frac{1}{2}[ABCD]$$
$$= \frac{1}{8}[ABCD]$$
$$= 30.$$

Similarly, since $CH = 4HD$, $DH = \frac{1}{5}CD$ and thus

$$[HDI] = \frac{1}{2} \times \frac{1}{2} \times \frac{1}{5}[ABCD]$$
$$= \frac{1}{20}[ABCD]$$
$$= 12.$$

For $\triangle JEH$ note JH is $\frac{1}{2} - \frac{1}{5} = \frac{3}{10}$ of CD, so

$$[JEH] = \frac{1}{2} \times 1 \times \frac{3}{10}[ABCD]$$
$$= \frac{3}{20}[ABCD]$$
$$= 36.$$

Hence, as $[AEJD] = [ABCD] \div 2 = 120$,

$$[EHI] = [AEJD] - [AEI] - [HDI] - [JEH]$$
$$= 120 - 30 - 12 - 36$$
$$= 42.$$

Finally, as F and G split BC in three equal segments,

$$[EFG] = \frac{1}{2} \times \frac{1}{3} \times \frac{1}{2}[ABCD]$$
$$= \frac{1}{12}[ABCD]$$
$$= 20$$

Therefore $[EHI] + [EFG] = 42 + 20 = 62$.

Answer: 62

Problem 13 Solution
Of James's 90 marbles, currently

$$\frac{2}{2+3+4} \times 90 = \frac{2}{9} \times 90 = 20 \text{ are blue,}$$
$$\frac{3}{2+3+4} \times 90 = \frac{3}{9} \times 90 = 30 \text{ are red,}$$
$$\text{and } \frac{4}{2+3+4} \times 90 = \frac{4}{9} \times 90 = 40 \text{ are green.}$$

Since James does not buy additional blue marbles, for $\frac{1}{18}$ of his marbles to be blue, he must have $20 \times 18 = 360$ marbles in total, which is $360 - 90 = 270$ additional marbles.

The packs come with $1 + 2 = 3$ marbles, so James buys $270 \div 3 = 90$ packs. Hence he ends up with

$$30 + 90 \times 1 = 120 \text{ red marbles,}$$
$$\text{and } 40 + 90 \times 2 = 220 \text{ green marbles.}$$

The ratio of blue to red to green marbles is thus

$$20 : 120 : 220 = 1 : 6 : 11$$

so $P^2 + Q^2 + R^2 = 1 + 36 + 121 = 158$.

Answer: 158

2.5 ZIML February 2019 Division M

Problem 14 Solution
If Aaron picks one of 19, 20, 21, 22, 23, 0, or 1, it won't matter what number Bert picks, they will meet between the desired time. The probability that Aaron picks one of these numbers is $\frac{7}{24}$.

If Aaron picks 18 and Bert picks one of $31,\ldots,59$, or if Aaron picks 2 and Bert picks one of $0,\ldots,30$, they will also meet at the desired time. The probability that they pick these numbers is $\frac{1}{24} \times \frac{29}{60} + \frac{1}{24} \times \frac{31}{60} = \frac{1}{24}$.

Therefore, the probability that they will meet online between 6:31 PM and 2:30 AM is $\frac{7}{24} + \frac{1}{24} = \frac{1}{3}$. Thus $Q - P = 3 - 1 = 2$.

Answer: 2

Problem 15 Solution
Recall all 8 faces of a regular octahedron are equilateral triangles. Since the surface area of the octahedron is $8\sqrt{3}$, each of the 8 faces has area $\sqrt{3} = \frac{\sqrt{3}}{4} \times 2^2$, thus, the side length of each of the faces of the octahedron is 2.

Since an octahedron has 12 edges, the sum of the lengths of all 12 edges is $2 \times 12 = 24$.

Answer: 24

Problem 16 Solution

First arrange the red and blue cards in a circle. Since there are $3+5=8$ cards in total, this can be done in $\frac{8!}{8} = 7! = 5040$ ways.

These 8 cards create 8 different spaces for the black cards. We can use 4 of these 8 spaces to place the black cards. This can be done in $\binom{8}{4} = 70$ ways.

Therefore, there are $5040 \times 70 = 352800$ different ways to arrange the cards in a circle.

Answer: 352800

Problem 17 Solution

Driving 550 miles at an average of 50 miles per hour means that, in total, Robert spent $550 \div 50 = 11$ hours in total on his trip.

He stopped for $20+15+35 = 70$ minutes, or $\frac{7}{6}$ hours. Therefore Robert spent
$$11 - \frac{7}{6} = \frac{59}{6}$$
hours actually driving, so his average speed without the stops was
$$550 \div \frac{59}{6} = \frac{3300}{59} \approx 55.93.$$
Rounded to the nearest tenth this is 55.9.

Answer: 55.9

Problem 18 Solution

To win more money than he paid for entering the game, Joel needs to win 9 dollars or more.

Out of the $6 \times 6 = 36$ possible outcomes of the pair of dice, there are 4 that add up to 9 ($(3,6), (4,5), (5,4)$ and $(6,3)$), 3 that add up to 10, 2 that add up to 11, and 1 that adds up to 12.

Therefore, the probability that he wins more money than what he paid for is $\dfrac{4+3+2+1}{36} = \dfrac{5}{18}$. Thus $P+Q = 18+5 = 23$.

Answer: 23

Problem 19 Solution

Connect AC, then $\triangle ABC$ is an isosceles triangle with $\angle ABC = 60°$, so it is in fact an equilateral triangle as shown below.

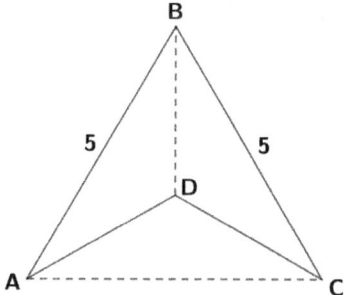

Further, as $\angle BCD = \angle DAB = 30°$, we in fact have $\triangle BCD$, $\triangle DAB$, and $\triangle CAD$ are all congruent triangles (with angles of $30°$, $30°$, and $120°$).

Therefore quadrilateral $ABCD$ has area $\dfrac{2}{3}$ of $\triangle ABC$, that is,

$$\frac{2}{3} \times \frac{5^2 \sqrt{3}}{4} = \frac{25\sqrt{3}}{6}.$$

Hence $P+Q+R = 25+3+6 = 34$.

Answer: 34

Problem 20 Solution

Finding a pattern for the last two digits of $15^1, 15^2, 15^3$ we get

$$15, 25, 75, 25, 75, \ldots$$

so after the first term it repeats $25, 75$ over and over.

Therefore pairing up 15^2 and 15^3, then 15^4 and 15^5, up to 15^8 and 15^9 we see their last two digits each add up to 100.

Hence the last two digits of our sum is the last two digits of 15^1 and 15^{10} which is $15 + 25 = 40$.

Answer: 40

2.6 ZIML March 2019 Division M

Below are the solutions from the Division M ZIML Competition held in March 2019.
The problems from the contest are available on p.59.

Problem 1 Solution
Since 3 workers can decorate 10 cupcakes in 5 minutes, $6 = 3 \times 2$ workers can decorate $10 \times 2 = 20$ workers in 5 minutes. Thus, the 6 workers would need $200 \div 20 \times 5 = 50$ minutes to decorate 200 cupcakes.

Answer: 50

Problem 2 Solution
Since Donna has 40 books in total, $40 - 22 = 18$ of the books are not geometry books, and $40 - 15 = 25$ do not have yellow covers.

We know 16 of the books do not have yellow covers and are not geometry books, so there are $25 - 16 = 9$ geometry books that do not have a yellow cover. Thus, there are $22 - 9 = 13$ yellow geometry books.

Answer: 13

Problem 3 Solution
Clearly the area of the shaded region is equal to the area of a semicircle with radius 4, minus the area of a semicircle with radius 3 and a semicircle with radius 1.

Thus, the shaded region has area

$$\frac{1}{2}\left(4^2\pi - \left(3^2\pi + 1^2\pi\right)\right) = 3\pi.$$

Therefore $K = 3$.

Answer: 3

Problem 4 Solution

The mean of the numbers is

$$(5 \times 5 + 6 \times 6 + 5 \times 7) \div 16 = 6,$$

and the mode is also 6.

If we add 7 to the list the mean would be equal to

$$(5 \times 5 + 6 \times 6 + 6 \times 7) \div 17 \approx 6.06,$$

however there would be two modes: 6 and 7. So the mean is not greater than both of the modes.

Thus the smallest positive integer that we can add to make the mean be greater than the mode (or modes) is 8.

Answer: 8

Problem 5 Solution

If all cupcakes have had 3 cherries, there would have been $3 \times 43 = 129$ cherries used in total. That is $187 - 129 = 58$ less cherries than she actually received. Since a 5-cherry cupcakes uses $5 - 3 = 2$ more cherries, $58 \div 2 = 29$ of the cupcakes had 5 cherries, and $43 - 29 = 14$ cupcakes had 3 cherries.

Thus, Lois spent $14 \times 2.50 + 29 \times 3.50 = 136.50$ dollars in her cupcakes.

Answer: 136.5

Problem 6 Solution

Let $\overline{ab}$ be the number we are looking for. Then we have $\overline{ab} = \overline{ba} - 27$, that is

$$10a + b = 10b + a - 27$$

and hence $9(b-a) = 27$ so $b - a = 3$.

Hence, we are looking for the smallest number $\overline{ab}$ such that $b - a = 3$, that is, the number is 14.

Answer: 14

Problem 7 Solution

Each of the isosceles triangles can be broken down into two congruent right triangles, as shown below.

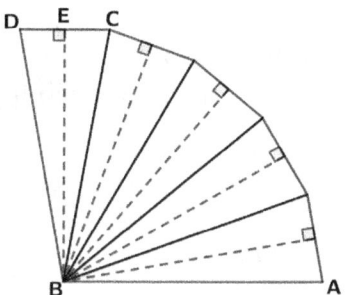

Since $\overline{AB} \parallel \overline{CD}$, $\overline{AB}$ is perpendicular to $\overline{BE}$. Hence, 9 of the small angles in the right triangles form a $90°$ angle, so each angle is $90° \div 9 = 10°$.

Therefore the small angle in each isosceles triangle is $2 \times 10° = 20°$. Thus the largest angles are each $(180° - 20°) \div 2 = 80°$.

Answer: 80

Problem 8 Solution

Since the hot water faucet pours 5 gallons per minute, and can fill the tub in 16 minutes, the bathtub can hold $5 \times 16 = 80$ gallons of water.

Note the drain can drain as much water as the cold water faucet, so during the first 8 minutes it was as if the drain was closed and only the hot water faucet was open, so the tub is exactly half full.

To fill in the remaining $80 \div 2 = 40$ gallons of water after closing the drain, Andy needs to leave both faucets open for $40 \div (3 + 5) = 5$ more minutes.

Answer: 5

Problem 9 Solution

There are 6^3 total outcomes. There are 4 outcomes (3, 4, 5 or 6) for each roll greater than 2, so there are 4^3 outcomes with each roll greater than 2. Therefore the probability is

$$\frac{4^3}{6^3} = \left(\frac{2}{3}\right)^3 = \frac{8}{27}.$$

and $Q - P = 27 - 8 = 19$.

Answer: 19

Problem 10 Solution

The first jar is 3 ounces of vinaigrette with a 1 : 3 ratio of vinegar to olive oil. Thus it is $3 \times \frac{1}{4} = \frac{3}{4}$ ounces vinegar and $3 \times \frac{3}{4} = \frac{9}{4}$ ounces olive oil.

A similar calculation for the second jar gives

$$6 \times \frac{2}{5} = \frac{12}{5} \text{ and } 6 \times \frac{3}{5} = \frac{18}{5}$$

ounces of vinegar and olive oil.

2.6 ZIML March 2019 Division M

Thus after the jars are combined the ratio is

$$\left(\frac{3}{4} + \frac{12}{5}\right) : \left(\frac{9}{4} + \frac{18}{5}\right)$$
$$= \left(\frac{15}{20} + \frac{48}{20}\right) : \left(\frac{45}{20} + \frac{72}{20}\right)$$
$$= (15 + 48) : (45 + 72)$$
$$= 63 : 117$$
$$= 7 : 13.$$

Therefore $a + b = 7 + 13 = 20$.

Answer: 20

Problem 11 Solution
Since the number leaves a remainder of 2 when divided by 3, 4 and 5, two less than the number is divisible by 2, 3, and 5.

The LCM of 3, 4, and 5 is $3 \times 4 \times 5 = 60$, so we want two more than a multiple of 60. The largest multiple of 60 less than 1000 is $16 \times 60 = 960$ so our number is $960 + 2 = 962$.

Answer: 962

Problem 12 Solution
Consider the diagram below

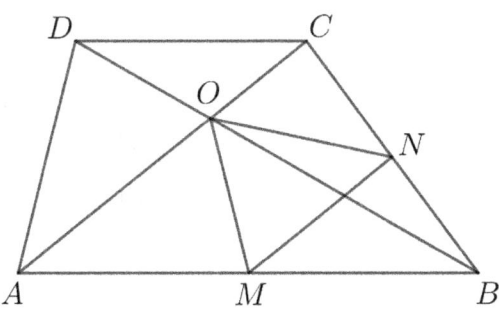

Let $[ABC]$ denote the area of $\triangle ABC$. Since M and N are the midpoints of AB and BC, we have $\triangle ABC \sim \triangle MBN$ with sides in ratio $2:1$. Thus, $[MBN] = \dfrac{1}{4}[ABC]$.

Note the height of $\triangle ABC$ is the same as the height of the trapezoid if we use AB as a base, thus $[ABC] = \dfrac{1}{2} \times 8 \times 4 = 16$, and $[MNB] = \dfrac{1}{4} \times 16 = 4$.

Using MN as a base, we can see $\triangle MNB$ and $\triangle MON$ have the same base and same height (since the height of MNB is half of the height from vertex B of ABC), hence they have the same area.

Therefore the area of $\triangle MON$ is 4.

Answer: 4

Problem 13 Solution

In the 3 seconds Paul is running before Russell starts, Paul runs $8 \times 3 = 24$ meters. Since Russell runs $9.5 - 8 = 1.5$ m/s faster than Paul, it therefore takes him $24 \div 1.5 = 16$ seconds to catch up. Thus Russell (and hence Paul as well) runs $16 \times 9.5 = 152$ meters.

Answer: 152

Problem 14 Solution

It is possible to calculate the prime factorization of
$$11^3 - 7^3 = 1331 - 343 = 988$$
directly. However, factoring (the difference of two cubes) gives
$$11^3 - 7^3 = (11-7)(11^2 + 11 \times 7 + 7^2)$$
$$= 4 \times 247$$
$$= 2^2 \times 13 \times 19.$$

Therefore the number has $(2+1)(1+1)(1+1) = 12$ factors.

Answer: 12

Problem 15 Solution

Dan has $3+4+3 = 10$ cards in total. They all have different symbols, so each is different. He can therefore choose 2 of them in $\binom{10}{2} = 45$ ways.

We subtract off the ways Dan does not get two cards of different colors. There are $\binom{3}{2} = 3$ ways to choose both cards blue, $\binom{4}{2} = 6$ ways to choose both cards red, and $\binom{3}{2} = 3$ ways to choose both cards yellow.

Thus, there are $45 - (3+6+3) = 33$ ways to pick two cards of different color.

Answer: 33

Problem 16 Solution

A number is a multiple of 45 if and only if it is a multiple of 5 and 9.

For the number to be a multiple of 9 we need the sum of the digits to be a multiple of 9, thus

$$a+2+0+1+9+b = a+b+12$$

must be a multiple of 9.

For the number to be a multiple of 5, it must end in 0 or 5. If $b = 0$, then $a+12$ is a multiple of 9, and so $a = 6$. This gives the number 620190. If $b = 5$, then $a+17$ is a multiple of 9, and so $a = 1$. This gives a second number 120195.

Therefore, the sum of all numbers of the form $\overline{a2019b}$ that are divisible by 45 is $620190 + 120195 = 740385$.

Answer: 740385

Problem 17 Solution

Without touching the fence with his leash, Percy can run freely in a sector with radius 20 feet open to an angle of 30°.

If Percy tries to go to the opposite side of the left fence, his leash would get stuck at the tree on the left and would only allow him to run in a semicircle with radius $20 - 15 = 5$ feet, as shown on the diagram.

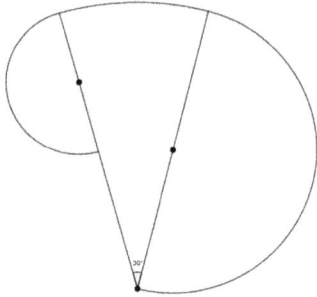

Similarly, if he tries to go to the opposite side of the right fence, he can run inside of a semicircle with radius $20 - 10 = 10$.

Altogether, the area in which Percy can run is

$$\frac{20^2\pi}{12} + \frac{5^2\pi}{2} + \frac{10^2\pi}{2} = \frac{575}{6}\pi$$

square feet. Therefore $A + B = 575 + 6 = 581$.

Answer: 581

2.6 ZIML March 2019 Division M

Problem 18 Solution

The first two friends start by saying 1 and 1. The next friend therefore says $1 + 1 = 2$. The next number is 0, because $1 + 2 = 3$ which has remainder of 0 when divided by 3.

Continuing the pattern first 8 numbers said are

$$1, 1, 2, 0, 2, 2, 1, 0.$$

After this, the pattern repeats (since $0 + 1 = 1$ and then $1 + 0 = 1$) with these same 8 numbers over and over.

Since the friends all say the same numbers, the number of people must be a multiple of 8. The smallest number of people possible greater than 10 is therefore $8 \times 2 = 16$.

Answer: 16

Problem 19 Solution

To buy a chocolate bar Justin would need two quarters. Thus, we have 3 cases, depending on if he bought 0, 1, or 2 chocolate bars.

If he bought 0 chocolate bars, he has 4 quarters available to buy the 5 different candies. Using stars and bars we can see there are exactly $\binom{4+5-1}{5-1} = 70$ ways for him to choose which candies to buy.

Similarly, there are $\binom{2+5-1}{5-1} = 15$ ways to choose the candies if he buys 1 chocolate bar, and $\binom{0+5-1}{5-1} = 1$ way to choose the candies if he bought 2 chocolate bars.

Altogether Justin can decide how to buy his candies in

$$70 + 15 + 1 = 86$$

different ways.

Answer: 86

Problem 20 Solution
Consider the following diagram.

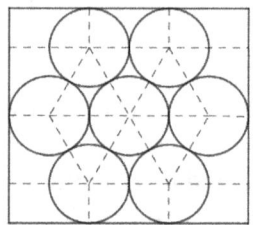

From the diagram we can see the length of the rectangle is 6 times the radius of the circles, and the width of the rectangle is 2 times the radius of the circles plus two times the height of an equilateral triangle with side length twice the radius of the circles.

Thus, the length of the rectangle is $6 \times 1 = 6$, and the width of the rectangle is $2 + 2 \times \sqrt{3}$, and the area of the rectangle is $6 \times (2 + 2 \times \sqrt{3}) = 12 + 12\sqrt{3}$.

Therefore $A + B + C = 12 + 12 + 3 = 27$.

Answer: 27

2.7 ZIML April 2019 Division M

Below are the solutions from the Division M ZIML Competition held in April 2019.
The problems from the contest are available on p.67.

Problem 1 Solution
Richard would work for a total of $3 + 4 + 5 = 12$ days. For the average during those 12 days to be 20 pages per day, he would need the total number of pages he wrote to be $12 \times 20 = 240$.

So far he has written $3 \times 10 + 15 \times 4 = 90$ pages, so he needs to write $240 - 90 = 150$ pages during the remaining 5 days, that is, $150 \div 5 = 30$ pages each day.

Answer: 30

Problem 2 Solution
From the list of numbers, 71, 73 and 79 are prime numbers, so each of them has 2 factors.

Factoring the others, $75 = 3 \times 5^2$ and $77 = 7 \times 11$, so 75 has $(1+1)(2+1) = 6$ factors, and 77 has $(1+1)(1+1) = 4$ factors.

Thus, among the numbers in the list, the one with the most factors is 75.

Answer: 75

Problem 3 Solution
The 70% of 32 is $32 \times 0.7 = 22.4$, which is not an integer, so at least 23 people do not like chocolate. Note we round up since 22 people make about 68% of her classmates.

Answer: 23

Problem 4 Solution

Recall the volume of a prism is $V = B \times h$, where B is the area of its base and h is its height, and the volume of a pyramid is $V = \frac{1}{3} \times B \times h$, where B is the area of its base and h is its height.

Since the pyramid and the box have the same base and the same height, the volume of the box is exactly 3 times the volume of the pyramid. Thus the volume of the prism is $3 \times 15 = 45$, so the volume of the Styrofoam cushioning is $45 - 15 = 30$ cubic inches.

Answer: 30

Problem 5 Solution

Recall that the product of the least common multiple and the greatest common divisor of a number is equal to the product of the two numbers. Thus, the second number is equal to $\frac{144 \times 24}{48} = 72$.

Answer: 72

Problem 6 Solution

To buy the 92 bottles of sparkling water buying the least amount of packs, we need to buy as many as the largest pack as possible. $92 \div 24 \approx 3.8$, so we need to buy 3 packs of 24 bottles, leaving $92 - 3 \times 24 = 20$ bottles remaining.

Since $20 \div 8 = 2.5$, we need 2 packs of 8 bottles, leaving $20 - 2 \times 8 = 4$ bottles remaining. Hence we need 1 pack of 4 bottles.

Therefore, to buy exactly 92 bottles of sparkling water, we need to buy at least $3 + 2 + 1 = 6$ packs.

Answer: 6

Problem 7 Solution

Let's pretend Carly ate 2 more pepperoni pizzas. So, she ate $19+2 = 21$ pizzas in total, and the ratio of pepperoni pizzas to veggie pizzas is $1:2$.

Thus, Carly ate
$$\frac{2}{1+2} \times 21 = 14$$
veggie pizzas last month.

Answer: 14

Problem 8 Solution

Since the sixth term of the sequence is 42, and the fifth term is 26, the fourth term is $42 - 26 = 16$.

Similarly, the third term of the sequence is $26 - 16 = 10$. The third term of the sequence is the sum of the first two, so the answer is 10.

Answer: 10

Problem 9 Solution

The sum of all the numbers in the die is $2+3+5+7 = 17$. Thus, the possible sums we can obtain by adding up the visible faces of the die are $17-2 = 15$, $17-3 = 14$, $17-5 = 12$, and $17-7 = 10$. Among these, only 12 is a multiple of 4.

Thus, the probability that the sum of the numbers on the visible faces of the cube is a multiple of 4 is $\frac{1}{4}$, so $Q - P = 4 - 1 = 3$.

Answer: 3

Problem 10 Solution

They can choose which 2 appetizers to get in $\binom{6}{2} = 15$ different ways. If Alan orders first, then Beatrice, and then Carol, Alan has 8 entrees to choose from, Beatrice has 7 entrees to choose from, and Charlie has 6 entrees to choose from.

Thus, they can choose to order their meal in $15 \times 8 \times 7 \times 6 = 5040$ different ways.

Answer: 5040

Problem 11 Solution

The prime factorization of a perfect square is made up entirely of even powers, so we need the prime factorization of $\sqrt{1350 \times K}$ to have exponents that are all multiples of 2. Thus $1350 \times K$ must have exponents that are all multiples of 4.

$1350 = 2 \times 3^3 \times 5^2$, so for $\sqrt{1350 \times K}$ (with K as small as possible) we need the prime factorization of K to be $2^3 \times 3 \times 5^2$, so $1350 \times K = 2^4 \times 3^4 \times 5^4$. That is, the smallest possible value of K is $K = 600$.

Answer: 600

Problem 12 Solution

Each of the interior angles of a regular nonagon is

$$\frac{180° \times (9-2)}{9} = 140°,$$

and each of the interior angles of a regular hexagon is

$$\frac{180° \times (6-2)}{6} = 120°.$$

Therefore, the marked angle is $140° - 120° = 20°$.

Answer: 20

2.7 ZIML April 2019 Division M

Problem 13 Solution

As the first carton holds 16 ounces and is 75% real orange juice, it contains
$$16 \times 75\% = 16 \times \frac{3}{4} = 12$$
ounces of real orange juice. Similarly, the other carton contains
$$10 \times 90\% = 9$$
ounces of real orange juice.

Thus, after mixing the two cartons of orange juice, Patrick has $16 + 10 = 26$ ounces of orange juice, of which $12 + 9 = 21$ ounces are real orange juice. Therefore, the orange juice mix is
$$\frac{21}{26} \approx 0.807 \approx 80.7\%$$
real orange juice. Thus rounded to the nearest integer, $P = 81$.

Answer: 81

Problem 14 Solution

A number is divisible by 15 if it is divisible by 3 and by 5.

Since the number $\overline{a34b}$ is divisible by 5, b is either 0 or 5, and since it is divisible by 3, the sum of its digits is a multiple of 3. If $b = 0$, the sum of the digits of the number is $a + 3 + 4 + 0 = a + 7$, so the least possible value of a that makes this a multiple of 3 is $a = 2$.

If $b = 5$, the sum of the digits of the number is $a + 3 + 4 + 5 = a + 12$, so the least possible value of a that makes this sum a multiple of 3 is $a = 3$.

Therefore, the least possible value of a is 2.

Answer: 2

Problem 15 Solution

As the new box is twice as long, twice as wide, and three times as high, we could fit $2 \times 2 \times 3 = 12$ smaller boxes in the larger box. (Arranged in 3 layers with 4 boxes per layer.)

Thus, the larger box can fit $250 \times 12 = 3000$ marbles.

Answer: 3000

Problem 16 Solution

To find numbers that are multiples of 2 and 3, but not 5, we need to find all numbers that are multiples of $2 \times 3 = 6$, except for the ones that are multiples of $2 \times 3 \times 5 = 30$.

As $200 \div 6 \approx 33.3$, there are 33 multiples of 6 between 1 and 200, and since $200 \div 30 \approx 6.6$, there are 6 multiples of 30 from 1 to 200. Thus, there are $33 - 6 = 27$ numbers between 1 and 200 that are multiple of 2 and 3, but not 5.

Answer: 27

Problem 17 Solution

Consider the labeled diagram below.

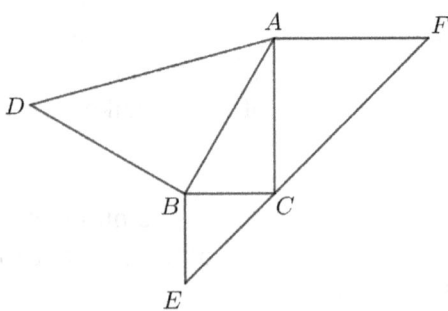

Let $[ABC]$ denote the area of $\triangle ABC$. Then

$$[BCE] = \frac{2 \times 2}{2} = 2$$

$$[ABC] = \frac{2 \times 2\sqrt{3}}{2} = 2\sqrt{3}$$

$$[DBA] = \frac{4 \times 4}{2} = 8$$

$$[AFC] = \frac{2\sqrt{3} \times 2\sqrt{3}}{2} = 6.$$

So, the area of all four triangles combined is

$$2 + 8 + 6 + 2\sqrt{3} = 16 + 2\sqrt{3}.$$

Therefore, $A + B + C = 16 + 2 + 3 = 21$.

Answer: 21

Problem 18 Solution

Since we do not care who gets off at each stop, this problem is equivalent to placing 12 identical balls in 6 numbered boxes, so we can use stars and bars to count how many possible lists can be made. We need 12 stars and $6 - 1$ bars, so there are

$$\binom{12 + 6 - 1}{6 - 1} = 6188$$

different lists the bus driver could make.

Answer: 6188

Problem 19 Solution

The surface area of the figure will be equal to the surface area of all 8 cubes combined minus the area of the faces that were used to glue the cubes.

Each cube has 6 faces, each with an area of $3 \times 3 = 9$. There are 7 pairs of faces that were glued together, so the total surface area of the figure is

$$(8 \times 6 - 7 \times 2) \times 9 = 306.$$

Answer: 306

Problem 20 Solution

Among the 9 consecutive integers, there is exactly one of them with remainder 2 when divided by 5. This means if we arrange the original numbers in increasing order, the number in the middle of the list has remainder 2 when divided by 5.

To have the smallest possible sum in each row, column, and diagonal of the square, we need to have numbers that are as small as possible. The smallest 9 consecutive integers with middle number leaving a remainder of 2 are

$$3, 4, 5, 6, 7, 8, 9, 10, 11.$$

Thus the two 0s were originally 5 and 10, the two 1s 6 and 11, etc.

If the top left corner is 5, then the first row has sum $5 + 3 + 8 = 16$. However the smallest possible sum for the bottom row is $6 + 11 + 4 = 21$. Thus the top left corner must be 10. Filling in the squares we get

10	3	8
5	7	9
6	11	4

where the sum of every row, column, and diagonal is 21.

Answer: 21

2.8 ZIML May 2019 Division M

Below are the solutions from the Division M ZIML Competition held in May 2019.
The problems from the contest are available on p.75.

Problem 1 Solution
Let's pretend Aiden ate 10 more green grapes. Then he ate $98 + 10 = 108$ grapes in total and the ratio of green grapes to purple grapes is $5 : 1$. This means he ate $108 \div (1 + 5) = 18$ purple grapes.

Answer: 18

Problem 2 Solution
Consider $\triangle CGI$ in the diagram below.

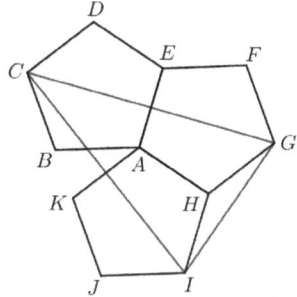

CG is the angle bisector of $\angle FGH$, so $\angle CGH = 108 \div 2 = 54$ degrees, and $\angle CGI = 54 + 18 = 72$ degrees.

$\triangle CGI$ is isosceles with $CG = CI$, so $\angle ICG = 180 - 2 \times 72 = 36$ degrees.

Answer: 36

Problem 3 Solution

A number is a multiple of both 15 and 18 if it is a multiple of their least common multiple. We can factor $15 = 3 \times 5$ and $18 = 2 \times 3^2$, so the LCM of 15 and 18 is $2 \times 3^2 \times 5 = 90$.

The prime factorization of any perfect square contains only even powers of numbers. Thus, the smallest perfect square that is a multiple of 90 is $2^2 \times 3^2 \times 5^2 = 900$.

Answer: 900

Problem 4 Solution

Since every day she does 2 more sit ups than the day before, the number of sit ups per day form an arithmetic sequence that starts with 5 and has common difference 2.

Since she does this for 2 full weeks, the last day she will do $5 + 13 \times 2 = 31$ sit ups. Therefore, after 14 days she will do $\dfrac{(5+31) \times 14}{2} = 252$ sit ups.

Answer: 252

Problem 5 Solution

There are $3 + 4 + 5 = 12$ cards in total, so there are $\binom{12}{2} = 66$ ways to choose two of them.

There are $\binom{3}{2} = 3$ ways to choose both of them green, $\binom{4}{2} = 6$ ways to choose both of them blue, and $\binom{5}{2} = 10$ ways to choose both of them red. Thus, there are $66 - (3 + 6 + 10) = 47$ ways to choose two cards of different color.

Therefore, the probability that the chosen cards have different color is $\dfrac{47}{66}$. Thus, $Q - P = 66 - 47 = 19$.

Answer: 19

Problem 6 Solution

After he refills his cup of coffee, $\dfrac{1}{2} \times \dfrac{1}{4} = \dfrac{1}{8}$ of his cup is milk, and the rest is coffee. Thus, the ratio of coffee to milk in his cup is $7 : 1$. Therefore, $a \times b = 7 \times 1 = 7$.

Answer: 7

Problem 7 Solution

Since the first time Dante gave away candy he got 6 candies left over, he must have given candy to 7 or more of his friends.

If Dante gave away candy to 7 of his friends, that would mean the bag contained $3 \times 7 + 6 = 27$ candies (since that is the only number of the form $7k + 6$ strictly between 20 and 30), but 27 is not divisible by 6.

Similarly, If Dante gave away candy to 8 of his friends, the bag would have $2 \times 8 + 6 = 22$ candies, but 22 is not divisible by 7.

If he gave away candy to 9 of his friends, the bag would have $2 \times 9 + 6 = 24$ candies. 24 is divisible by 8, so this the number of candies in Dante's bag.

Answer: 24

Problem 8 Solution

Working together, they folded half of the clothes in 15 minutes, so it would have taken them 30 minutes to fold all of the clothes together. Thus in one minute they can fold $\frac{1}{30}$ of the clothes.

Since Roy can fold all of his clothes in 50 minutes, in one minute he can fold $\frac{1}{50}$ of his clothes. Hence, in one minute, Scottie could fold $\frac{1}{30} - \frac{1}{50} = \frac{1}{75}$ of the clothes. This means it would take Scottie 75 minutes to fold all of Roy's clothes all by himself.

Answer: 75

Problem 9 Solution

The side length of the small squares is the same as the length of the legs of the isosceles right triangles, and the side length of the big square is the same as the length of the hypotenuse of the isosceles right triangle. Thus, the area of each small square is 2 times the area of the isosceles right triangle, and the area of the big square is 4 times the area of the isosceles right triangle, as pictured on the diagram below.

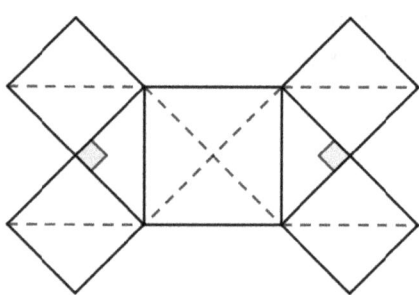

Hence, the area of the entire figure is $(2+4\times 2+4)\times 8 = 112$.

Answer: 112

Problem 10 Solution

Since they run at the same constant speed and start running at diametrically opposite points on the track, by the first time they meet, each has run $\frac{1}{4}$ of a full lap around the track. From this point, every time they meet they have run $\frac{1}{2}$ of a full lap more than they had run the previous time they met.

This way, by the 5th time they meet they've ran $\frac{1}{4}+4\times\frac{1}{2}=\frac{9}{4}$ of a lap. Since $\frac{1}{4}$ of a lap is 150 meters, they each have run $9\times 150 = 1350$ meters.

Answer: 1350

Problem 11 Solution

Consider the line segments joining the intersection points of the circles.

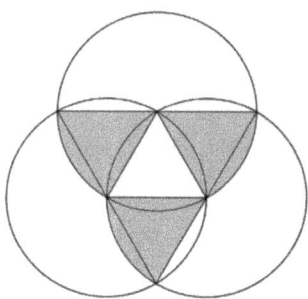

Rearranging the shaded regions we can see each of them has the same area as a circular sector that is $\frac{1}{6}$ of a circle.

Thus, the combined area of the three shaded regions is $\frac{1}{2}$ of the area of one circle, that is $\frac{1}{2} \times 16\pi = 8\pi$. Therefore, $K = 8$.

Answer: 8

Problem 12 Solution

The numbers 2, 3, 5, 7, and 11 have exactly 2 factors since they are prime. The numbers $4 = 2^2$, and $9 = 3^2$ each have 3 factors. Lastly, the numbers $6 = 2 \times 3$, $8 = 2^3$, and $10 = 2 \times 5$ each have 4 factors.

Therefore, Ms. Keaton's students formed 3 groups.

Answer: 3

Problem 13 Solution

Let's first figure out how many regular vehicles and how many vehicles towing a 1 wheel trailer entered the parking lot.

If all 51 vehicles had been regular vehicles, Russ would have counted $51 \times 4 = 204$ wheels in total. Since he counted $230 - 204 = 26$ more wheels than that, and each vehicle towing a 2 wheel trailer increases the wheel count by 2, there were $26 \div 2 = 13$ vehicles towing a 2 wheel trailer and $51 - 13 = 38$ regular vehicles entering the parking lot.

Therefore, during his shift Russ received $38 \times 15 + 13 \times 20 = 830$ dollars.

Answer: 830

Problem 14 Solution

Since Stacey walks north and Tracy walks east, the paths they followed can be regarded as the legs of a right triangle.

Observe $24 = 6 \times 4$ and $18 = 6 \times 3$. Since $(3,4,5)$ is a Pythagorean triple, so is $(18, 24, 30)$, so the distance between Stacey and Tracy is 30 meters.

Answer: 30

Problem 15 Solution

Since $P(1) = 20\%$, $P(3) = 30\%$, $P(5) = 25\%$, and $P(2) = P(4) = P(6)$, we have $P(2) = (100\% - (20\% + 30\% + 25\%)) \div 3 = 8.\overline{3}\%$.

Thus, the probability of picking a prime number is $P(2) + P(3) + P(5) = 8.\overline{3}\% + 30\% + 25\% \approx 63.3\%$.

Answer: 63.3

Problem 16 Solution

$\gcd(B,C) = 6$ so we know B and C are both multiples of 2 and 3.

$$\text{lcm}(A, C) = 1800 = 2^3 \times 3^2 \times 5^2,$$

so either A or C is a multiple of each of 8, 9, and 25. We know B is a multiple of 3, yet $\gcd(A, B) = 20$, which is not a multiple of 3. Therefore A is not a multiple of 3 and hence C must be the multiple of 9.

Since C is a multiple of 2 and 9, C is a multiple of 18. If $A = 2^3 \times 5^2 = 200$ and $B = \text{lcm}(20, 6) = 60$, then $C = 18$ works, with $\gcd(A,B) = 20$, $\gcd(B,C) = 6$, and $\text{lcm}(A,C) = 1800$. Therefore 18 is the smallest possible value of C.

Answer: 18

Problem 17 Solution

First decide the order in which the families as a group will stand in line for the picture. There are 3 families, so they can decide this order in $3! = 6$ ways.

Then decide the order in which each of the families will stand for the picture. The Spears can be arranged in $4! = 24$ ways, the Atkinsons in $3! = 6$ ways, and the Lockwoods in $3! = 6$ ways.

Therefore, they can arrange themselves in line for a picture in $6 \times 24 \times 6 \times 6 = 5184$ ways.

Answer: 5184

Problem 18 Solution

From the diagram we can see the side lengths of the bases of the pyramids add up to 6. We also know that the side length of the larger one is twice the smaller one, so they have side length 2 and 4.

Thus, the combined volume of the pyramids is

$$\frac{2^2 \times 2}{3} + \frac{4^2 \times 2}{3} = \frac{40}{3}.$$

Rounded to the nearest tenth, the combined volume of the pyramids is 13.3.

Answer: 13.3

Problem 19 Solution

For $\dfrac{\sqrt{12n}}{14}$ to be a perfect square, we should have that

$$\left(\frac{\sqrt{12n}}{14}\right)^2 = \frac{12n}{14^2} = \frac{3n}{7^2}$$

2.8 ZIML May 2019 Division M

is a perfect fourth power.

For $\dfrac{3n}{7^2}$ to be an integer, we need $n = 7^2 \times k$ for some integer k, so $\dfrac{3n}{7^2} = 3k$. The smallest value of k that makes $3k$ a perfect fourth power is 3^3, so the smallest value of n that yields a perfect fourth power is $n = 3^3 \times 7^2 = 1323$.

Answer: 1323

Problem 20 Solution

Consider the sets C, D, and H that represent cat owners, dog owners and hamster owners, respectively.

We know there are 13 students that have dogs, and 7 of them also have a cat or a hamster, so $n(D) = 13$ and $n((C \cup H) \cap D) = 7$. Since $D = ((C \cup H) \cap D) \cup ((C^c \cap H^c) \cap D)$, $n((C^c \cap H^c) \cap D) = n(D) - n((C \cup H) \cap D) = 13 - 7 = 6$. So there are 6 students that have dogs but do not have cats nor hamsters at home.

Answer: 6

2.9 ZIML June 2019 Division M

Below are the solutions from the Division M ZIML Competition held in June 2019.
The problems from the contest are available on p.83.

Problem 1 Solution
If there were indeed 2 fewer 8 year olds, and 4 more 6 year olds, there would be $28 - 2 + 4 = 30$ kids, so $30 \div 3 = 10$ of each age group.

This means there are $10 + 2 = 12$ 8 year olds, 10 7 year olds, and $10 - 4 = 6$ 6 year olds.

Answer: 6

Problem 2 Solution
The whole shaded region fits inside a 6×6 square. The area of the shaded region is then the area of the square minus the area of four triangles, as pictured on the diagram below.

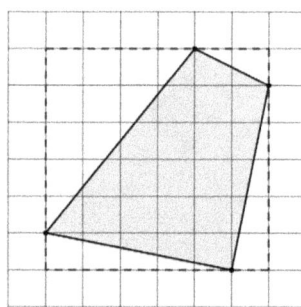

Thus, the area of the shaded region is

$$6 \times 6 - \left(\frac{1 \times 5}{2} + \frac{1 \times 5}{2} + \frac{1 \times 2}{2} + \frac{5 \times 4}{2} \right) = 20$$

square units.

Answer: 20

Problem 3 Solution

There are 10 males in the club. If 60% forget to bring their cookbook, then
$$60\% \times 10 = 6$$
males forgot their cookbook. Similarly
$$40\% \times 20 = 8$$
females forgot their cookbook. Hence $6+8 = 14$ of the $10+20 = 30$ members forgot their cookbook. If one is randomly chosen, the probability they forgot their cookbook is thus
$$\frac{14}{30} = \frac{7}{15}$$
and $Q - P = 15 - 7 = 8$.

Answer: 8

Problem 4 Solution

We can find the amount of money they received by working backwards.

Manny has now \$600, so before buying groceries he had
$$600 \div \frac{1}{2} = 1200$$
dollars. Thus, he originally received
$$1200 \div \left(1 - \frac{2}{3}\right) = 3600$$
dollars.

Therefore Larson also received $3600. After spending half of his money in groceries he was left with

$$3600 \times \frac{1}{2} = 1800$$

dollars, and after spending one third of that, he was left with

$$1800 \times \left(1 - \frac{1}{3}\right) = 1200$$

dollars.

Answer: 1200

Problem 5 Solution
Since $\overline{BD}$ is an altitude, both $\triangle ABD$ and $\triangle BCD$ are right triangles. Using the Pythagorean theorem,

$$AB^2 = AD^2 + BD^2$$
$$41 = AD^2 + 25$$
$$AD^2 = 16$$

so $AD = \sqrt{16} = 4$. Hence $CD = 6 - 4 = 2$. Using the Pythagorean theorem again we have

$$BC^2 = CD^2 + BD^2$$
$$BC^2 = 4 + 25$$
$$BC^2 = 29.$$

Therefore $BC = \sqrt{29}$ and $R = 29$.

Answer: 29

2.9 ZIML June 2019 Division M

Problem 6 Solution

Since 8 workers can finish the job in 30 hours, 4 workers can finish in $2 \times 30 = 60$ hours.

Thus, 4 workers working for 20 hours finish $\dfrac{20}{60} = \dfrac{1}{3}$ of the job.

When 4 more workers come join them, they are now a team of $4+4 = 8$ workers. Since they need to finish $\dfrac{2}{3}$ of the job, they would require $30 \times \dfrac{2}{3} = 20$ hours to finish the job.

Answer: 20

Problem 7 Solution

Since the number leaves a remainder of 5 when divided by 8, 9 and 10, it must be 5 more than a common multiple of 8, 9 and 10.

Any number that is a multiple of 8, 9 and 10 is a multiple of their LCM, 360.

Since $9999 \div 360 \approx 27.8$, the largest 4-digit number that is a multiple of 360 is $360 \times 27 = 9720$. Therefore, the number we are looking for is $9720 + 5 = 9725$.

Answer: 9725

Problem 8 Solution

Susan will press one key for each digit of the numbers she is adding, and the + key in between each two consecutive numbers.

From 1 to 200 there are 9 one-digit numbers, 90 two-digit numbers, and 101 three-digit numbers. So Susan will need to press $9 + 2 \times 90 + 3 \times 101 = 492$ keys for the digits, 199 times the + key and 1 time the = key. Thus, Susan will need to press

$492 + 199 + 1 = 692$ keys in total.

Answer: 692

Problem 9 Solution
Since the ratio of the number of red, blue and green candy is $1 : 3 : 5$, for every 5 green candies there are 3 blue candies and 1 red candy. There are $75 \div 5 = 15$ groups of $5 + 3 + 1 = 9$ candies, so there are $15 \times 9 = 135$ candies in the bowl.

Answer: 135

Problem 10 Solution
Ferdinand has balls of 3 different colors. Grouping them together, he could arrange them in a circle in $\dfrac{3!}{3} = 2!$ different ways. However, since each color group has multiple (distinct) balls, we need to multiple by 3!, 2! and 5! to order the balls. Thus there are

$$2! \times 3! \times 2! \times 5! = 2880$$

total arrangements.

Answer: 2880

Problem 11 Solution
Let $[ABC]$ denote the area of ABC. Using DC as base, $\triangle BCD$ has the same height as trapezoid $ABCD$. Since $[BCD] = 10$ and $DC = 5$, the height is $10 \times 2 \div 5 = 4$.

Using AB as base, $\triangle ABC$ has height 4 as well, and $[ABC] = [ABCD] - [BCD] = 34 - 10 = 24$, so $AB = 24 \times 2 \div 4 = 12$.

Answer: 12

Problem 12 Solution
To come back to the same step he started he needs to either go up and then down, or go down and then up.

The probability that he goes up and then down is $\frac{2}{3} \times \frac{1}{3} = \frac{2}{9}$. The probability that he goes down and then up is $\frac{1}{3} \times \frac{2}{3} = \frac{2}{9}$. Thus, the probability that he comes back to the same step after moving twice is $\frac{2}{9} + \frac{2}{9} = \frac{4}{9}$. Therefore, $Q - P = 9 - 4 = 5$.

Answer: 5

Problem 13 Solution

The number of students in Lance's class must be divisible by 7, 5 and 3, otherwise his observations could not be true.

The smallest number that is divisible by 7, 5, and 3 is $\text{lcm}(7, 5, 3) = 105$, so there must be 105 students in Lance's class.

Answer: 105

Problem 14 Solution

For each of the 6 friends in the group we have 6 possible choices, either they speak only one of the three languages (F, S, G), or they speak two of the three languages (F&S, F&G, S&G).

Therefore there are $6^6 = 46656$ different ways in which this situation could happen.

Answer: 46656

Problem 15 Solution

A view from the top shows that each layer of the chimney is built using 10 bricks.

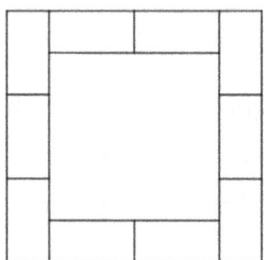

As the chimney is 10 bricks tall, $10 \times 10 = 100$ bricks were used to build the chimney.

Answer: 100

Problem 16 Solution
The prime factorization of 604800 is $2^7 \cdot 3^3 \cdot 5^2 \cdot 7$. Thus, the largest perfect square that divides 604800 is $2^6 \cdot 3^2 \cdot 5^2$, so the smallest value of n that makes $\dfrac{604800}{n}$ a perfect square is

$$\frac{2^7 \cdot 3^3 \cdot 5^2 \cdot 7}{2^6 \cdot 3^2 \cdot 5^2} = 2 \cdot 3 \cdot 7 = 42.$$

Answer: 42

Problem 17 Solution
Note all numbers in the set are of the form $3 + 4k$ for $k = 0, 1, \ldots, 5$.

The sum of three numbers $3 + 4k_1$, $3 + 4k_2$, $3 + 4k_3$ is $9 + 4(k_1 + k_2 + k_3)$, so there are as many different sums as there are sums of the form $k_1 + k_2 + k_3$ with $k_i = 0, 1, \ldots, 5$.

The smallest possible sum of the form $k_1 + k_2 + k_3$ is $0 + 1 + 2 = 3$, and the largest possible sum is $3 + 4 + 5 = 12$. Note all sums in between are also possible, Thus, there are $12 - 3 + 1 = 10$ distinct possible sums.

Answer: 10

Problem 18 Solution
Each of Ron's pieces is $8 \times 2 \times 2 = 32$ board feet, so they cost $35 \times 32 = 1120$ dollars each.

Therefore, Ron will pay $3 \times 1120 = 3360$ dollars for his wood.

Answer: 3360

Problem 19 Solution
The second week she will save $50 \times 1.2 = 60$ dollars; the third week she will save $60 \times 1.2 = 72$ dollars; the fourth week she will save $60 \times 1.2 = 86.4$, etc. We can summarize the amounts she saves each week in the following table.

Week	Saves ($)	Total
1	50	50
2	60	110
3	72	182
4	86.4	268.40
5	103.68	372.08
6	124.42	496.50

We can see that after 5 weeks she still has less than \$400 but by the 6th week she has more than \$400. Hence it takes 6 weeks for Dorothy to save the money.

Answer: 6

Problem 20 Solution
Recall if the prime factorization of a number is $p_1^{e_1} \cdots p_k^{e_k}$, then it has exactly $(e_1 + 1) \cdots (e_k + 1)$ factors.

The following table summarizes the number of factors for all numbers between 1 and 30.

form	numbers	# of factors
1	1	1
p	2, 3, 5, 7, 11, 13, 17, 19, 23, 29	$1+1=2$
p^2	4, 9, 25	$2+1=3$
p^3	8, 27	$3+1=4$
p^4	16	$4+1=5$
$p \cdot q$	6, 10, 14, 15, 21, 22, 26	$(1+1)(1+1)=4$
$p^2 \cdot q$	18, 20, 28	$(2+1)(1+1)=6$
$p^3 \cdot q$	24	$(3+1)(1+1)=8$
$p \cdot q \cdot r$	30	$(1+1)(1+1)(1+1)=8$

We can see the largest number of factors a number has is 8, so $n = 8$.

Answer: 8

3. Appendix

3.1 Division M Topics Covered

Pre-Algebra and Word Problems*

- Ratios and Proportions: Using ratios to find parts of a whole, Calculating missing information from proportional relationships, Direct and Inverse Proportions, etc.
- Percents: Calculating percent increases and decreases, Relationship between percents and ratios, Using percents in mixture problems (e.g. 40% water and 60% oil)
- Problem Solving Methods: Chicken and Rabbit method, Using ratios when given sums or differences,
- Motion Problems using (Speed)x(Time)=(Distance), Average Speed, Applying direct and inverse proportions to motion problems

- Work using (Rate)x(Time)=(Work Done), Average Rate of Work, Applying direct and inverse proportions to work problems

*Note: Setting up and solving equations is not necessary for any of the problems in Division M. Students are allowed to use equations to solve the questions, but the questions are designed to be solved without using equations or systems of equations.

Geometry

- Areas and Perimeters of Basic Shapes such as triangles, rectangles, parallelograms, trapezoids, and circles
- Angles in Parallel Lines (corresponding angles, alternating interior/exterior angles, same-side interior/exterior angles, etc.)
- Triangles: Congruence and Similarity, Pythagorean theorem, Ratios of Sides for triangles with angles of $45°, 45°, 90°$ or $30°, 60°, 90°$
- Interior and Exterior Angles of Polygons, including the sum of all the interior or exterior angles, the measure of each angle if the polygon is regular, etc.
- Geometric Reasoning with Areas: Congruent shapes have the same area, Similar triangles have a ratio of areas that is the square of the ratio of their sides, Triangles with the same height have a ratio of their areas equal to the ratio of their bases, etc.
- Circles: Arc Length, Sector Area, Definitions for Tangent Lines and Tangent Circles
- Volumes and Surface Areas of Basic Solids such as cubes, spheres, rectangular prisms (boxes), and pyramids

Counting and Probability

- Sum and Product Rules

3.1 Division M Topics Covered

- Permutations and Combinations
- Counting Methods: Complementary counting, Stars and bars (also called sticks and stones, balls and urns, etc.), Grouping objects that must be together, Inserting objects that must be apart into spaces between objects, etc.
- Sequences: Arithmetic and Geometric Sequences, Sum of elements in an arithmetic sequence, Finding patterns for general sequences
- Probability and Sets: Definitions for event, sample space, complement, intersection, and union, Understanding the use of Venn Diagrams
- Probability in Finite Sample Spaces: Probability as a ratio of outcomes, Probabilities sum to 1, Computing probabilities with complements
- Geometrical Probability: Probability as a ratio of lengths, areas, or volumes
- Basic Statistics: Mean (Average), Median, Mode for lists, Interpreting data from graphs, bar charts, tables, etc.

Number Theory

- Fundamental Definitions: Prime numbers, factors/divisors, multiples, least common multiple (LCM), greatest common factor/divisor (GCF or GCD), perfect squares/cubes/etc.
- Divisibility Rules for numbers such as 2, 3, 4, 5, 8, 9, 10, 11, and how to combine the rules for numbers such as 6, 22, etc.
- (Unique) Prime Factorization and using the prime factorization to find the number of factors, to test whether a number is a perfect square/cube/etc, to find the LCM or GCD, etc.
- Factoring Tricks: Factors come in pairs, perfect squares have an odd number of factors, etc.
- Remainders and Patterns: Finding the units digit, finding the last two digits, finding the remainder when divided by 11, etc.

- Basic Modular Arithmetic: Understand "congruent modulo m" means two numbers have the same remainder when divided by m, The sum of two numbers is congruent modulo m to the sum of the remainders of the numbers when divided by m

3.2 Glossary of Common Math Terms

Acute Angle An angle less than $90°$.

Altitude of a Triangle A line segment connecting a vertex of a triangle to the opposite side forming a right angle. Also called the height of a triangle.

Angle A figure formed by two rays sharing a common vertex. Often measured in degrees.

Arc The curve of a circle connecting two points.

Area The amount of space a region takes up. Often denoted using square brackets: area of $\triangle ABC = [ABC]$.

Arithmetic Sequence A sequence where the difference between one term and the next is constant.

Average See Mean.

Base of a Triangle One side of a triangle, often used when the altitude is drawn from the opposite side to this base.

Binomial Coefficient The symbol $\binom{n}{k} = \dfrac{n!}{k!(n-k)!}$.

Chord A line segment connecting two points on the outside of a circle.

Circle A round shape consisting of points that all have the same distance (called the radius) from the center of the circle.

Circumference The perimeter of a circle.

Composite Number A number that is not prime.

Congruent Two shapes or figures that are exactly the same.

Cube A solid figure formed by 6 congruent squares that all meet at right angles.

Deck of Cards A standard deck of cards has 52 cards. There are 4 suits (clubs, diamonds, hearts, and spades) with each suit having cards of 13 ranks (A (ace), $2, 3, \ldots, 10$, J (jack), Q (queen), and K (king)).

Denominator The bottom number in a fraction.

Diagonal A line segment connecting two vertices of a shape or solid that is not an edge of the shape or solid.

Diameter A chord passing through the center of a circle. The diameter has length that is twice the radius.

Die or Dice A standard die (plural is dice) has 6 sides. Each of the 6 sides has the same chance when the die is rolled.

Digit One of $0, 1, 2, \ldots, 9$ used when writing a number.

Distinguishable Objects Objects that are different.

Divisible A number is divisible by another number if there is no remainder when the first number is divided by the second. For example, 35 is divisible by 7.

Divisor A number that evenly divides another number. For example, 6 is a divisor of 48. Also called a factor.

Edge A line segment connecting two vertices on the outside of a shape or solid.

Equally Likely Having the same chance of occurring.

3.2 Glossary of Common Math Terms

Equiangular Polygon A shape with all equal angles.

Equilateral Polygon A shape with all equal sides.

Equilateral Triangle A regular triangle, one with three equal sides and three equal angles.

Even Number A number divisible by 2.

Exponent The number another number is raised to for powers. For example, in a to the power of b (a^b), the exponent is b.

Face The shape or polygon on the outside of a solid region.

Factor of a Number A number that evenly divides another number. For example, 6 is a factor of 48. Also called a divisor.

Factorial The symbol ! where $n! = n \times (n-1) \times (n-2) \cdots \times 1$.

Fraction An expression of a quotient. For example, $\frac{1}{2}$ or $\frac{9}{7}$.

Geometric Sequence A sequence where the ratio between one term and the next is constant.

Greatest Common Divisor/Factor (GCD/GCF) The largest number that is a divisor/factor of two or more numbers.

Indistinguishable Objects Objects that are the same.

Intersecting Lines or curves that cross each other.

Intersection of Two Sets The set of objects that are in both of the two sets. Denoted using ∩. For example, $\{2,3\} \cap \{3,4,5\} = \{3\}$.

Isosceles Triangle A triangle with two equal sides and two equal angles.

Least Common Multiple (LCM) The smallest number that is a multiple of two or more numbers.

Mean The sum of the numbers in a list divided by the how many numbers occur in the list. Also called the average.

Median The number in the middle of a list when the list is arranged in increasing order.

Midpoint The point in the middle of a line segment.

Mode The number or numbers occurring most often in a list of numbers.

Multiple A number that is an integer times another number. For example, 72 is a multiple of 8.

Numerator The top number in a fraction.

Obtuse Angle An angle between $90°$ and $180°$.

Odd Number A number not divisible by 2.

Parallel Lines Lines that do not intersect.

Perfect Cube A number that is another number cubed. For example, $64 = 4^3$ is a perfect cube.

Perfect Square A number that is another number squared. For example, $64 = 8^2$ is a perfect square.

Perimeter The length/distance around the outside of a shape.

3.2 Glossary of Common Math Terms

Pi (π) A number used often in geometry. $\pi = 3.1415926\ldots \approx 3.14 \approx \frac{22}{7}$.

Polygon A shape formed by connected line segments.

Prime Factorization The expression of a number as the product of all its prime factors. For example, 24 has prime factorization $2 \times 2 \times 2 \times 3 = 2^3 \times 3$.

Prime Number A number whose only factors are one and itself.

Proportional Ratios Ratios that have equal values when expressed in fraction form. For example, $2 : 3$ is proportional to $8 : 12$.

Quadrilateral A shape with four sides.

Quotient The integer quantity when dividing one number by another. For example, the quotient of $38 \div 5$ is 7 as $38 = 7 \times 5 + 3$.

Radius of a Circle The distance from the center of the circle to any point on the outside of the circle.

Randomly Chosen for a group of objects. Unless specified, the chance of choosing each object is the same as any other object.

Rank of a Card See Deck of Cards.

Ratio A relation depicting the relation between two quantities. For example $2 : 3$ or $\frac{2}{3}$ denotes that for every 3 of the second quantity there are 2 of the first quantity.

Rational Number A number that can be written as a fraction.

Copyright © ARETEEM INSTITUTE. All rights reserved.

Reciprocal One divided by the number. For example, the reciprocal of 7 is $\frac{1}{7}$.

Rectangle A quadrilateral with four right angles (an equiangular quadrilateral).

Regular Polygon A polygon with all equal sides and all equal angles (equilateral and equiangular).

Remainder The quantity left over when one integer is divided by another. For example, the remainder of $38 \div 5$ is 3 as $38 = 7 \times 5 + 3$.

Rhombus A quadrilateral with four equal sides (an equilateral quadrilateral).

Right Angle A $90°$ angle.

Right Triangle A triangle containing a right angle.

Scalene Triangle A triangle with three unequal sides and three unequal angles.

Sector The region formed by an arc and the two radii connecting the ends of the arc to the center of the circle.

Sequence An ordered list of numbers.

Set An unordered collection or group of objects without repeated elements. Denoted using curly brackets. For example, $\{1,2,3,4\}$ is the set containing the integers $1,\ldots,4$.

Similar Shapes or solids that have the same angles and sides that share a common ratio.

3.2 Glossary of Common Math Terms

Simplest Radical Form An expression containing a radical $\sqrt[n]{a}$ such that the radical does not appear in the denominator, and the number a inside the radical is an integer that has no perfect n^{th} power of a prime as a factor.

Sphere A round solid consisting of points that all have the same distance (called the radius) from the center of the sphere.

Square A shape with four equal sides and four equal angles (a regular quadrilateral).

Subset A set of objects that is contained inside a larger set of objects. Denoted using $\subseteq$. For example $\{2,3\} \subseteq \{1,2,3,4\}$.

Suit of a Card See Deck of Cards.

Surface Area The total area of all the faces of a solid.

Trapezoid A quadrilateral with one pair of parallel sides.

Triangle A shape with three sides.

Union of Two Sets The set of objects that are in one or both of the two sets. Denoted using $\cup$. For example, $\{2,3\} \cup \{3,4,5\} = \{2,3,4,5\}$.

Venn Diagram A diagram with circles used to understand the relationship between overlapping sets.

Vertex The intersection of line segments, especially the intersection of sides or edges in a shape or solid.

Volume The amount of space a solid region takes up.

With Replacement When choosing objects with replacement, a chosen object is returned to the others allowing it to be chosen more than once.

3.3 ZIML Answers

ZIML October 2018 Division M

Problem 1:	132	Problem 11:	2.5
Problem 2:	3	Problem 12:	150
Problem 3:	39	Problem 13:	210
Problem 4:	32	Problem 14:	117
Problem 5:	50	Problem 15:	11
Problem 6:	66	Problem 16:	604800
Problem 7:	21	Problem 17:	102
Problem 8:	1250	Problem 18:	368
Problem 9:	3.6	Problem 19:	3
Problem 10:	77.8	Problem 20:	5

ZIML November 2018 Division M

Problem 1:	9.5	Problem 11:	38.5
Problem 2:	2	Problem 12:	0.6
Problem 3:	7	Problem 13:	2479
Problem 4:	5400	Problem 14:	45
Problem 5:	86	Problem 15:	-27
Problem 6:	7722	Problem 16:	409
Problem 7:	100	Problem 17:	11340
Problem 8:	3069	Problem 18:	85
Problem 9:	12	Problem 19:	12
Problem 10:	9989	Problem 20:	1

ZIML December 2018 Division M

Problem 1:   1515

Problem 2:   152

Problem 3:   3

Problem 4:   2.2

Problem 5:   5

Problem 6:   36

Problem 7:   44

Problem 8:   21

Problem 9:   10

Problem 10: 480

Problem 11: 201840

Problem 12: 24

Problem 13: 37

Problem 14: 12

Problem 15: 100

Problem 16: 288

Problem 17: 55

Problem 18: 120

Problem 19: 61

Problem 20: 12.5

ZIML January 2019 Division M

Problem 1: 185

Problem 2: 1500

Problem 3: 68

Problem 4: 1960

Problem 5: 45

Problem 6: 2

Problem 7: 12

Problem 8: 5040

Problem 9: 28

Problem 10: 35721

Problem 11: 13

Problem 12: 124

Problem 13: 14400

Problem 14: 49.5

Problem 15: 30

Problem 16: 3600

Problem 17: 50

Problem 18: 0

Problem 19: 79992

Problem 20: 5

ZIML February 2019 Division M

Problem 1:   96

Problem 2:   42

Problem 3:   3.5

Problem 4:   1836

Problem 5:   331

Problem 6:   7

Problem 7:   6

Problem 8:   21

Problem 9:   52

Problem 10:   1584

Problem 11:   18

Problem 12:   62

Problem 13:   158

Problem 14:   2

Problem 15:   24

Problem 16:   352800

Problem 17:   55.9

Problem 18:   23

Problem 19:   34

Problem 20:   40

ZIML March 2019 Division M

Problem 1:	50	Problem 11:	962
Problem 2:	13	Problem 12:	4
Problem 3:	3	Problem 13:	152
Problem 4:	8	Problem 14:	12
Problem 5:	136.5	Problem 15:	33
Problem 6:	14	Problem 16:	740385
Problem 7:	80	Problem 17:	581
Problem 8:	5	Problem 18:	16
Problem 9:	19	Problem 19:	86
Problem 10:	20	Problem 20:	27

ZIML April 2019 Division M

Problem 1:	30	Problem 11:	600
Problem 2:	75	Problem 12:	20
Problem 3:	23	Problem 13:	81
Problem 4:	30	Problem 14:	2
Problem 5:	72	Problem 15:	3000
Problem 6:	6	Problem 16:	27
Problem 7:	14	Problem 17:	21
Problem 8:	10	Problem 18:	6188
Problem 9:	3	Problem 19:	306
Problem 10:	5040	Problem 20:	21

ZIML May 2019 Division M

Problem 1:   18

Problem 2:   36

Problem 3:   900

Problem 4:   252

Problem 5:   19

Problem 6:   7

Problem 7:   24

Problem 8:   75

Problem 9:   112

Problem 10: 1350

Problem 11: 8

Problem 12: 3

Problem 13: 830

Problem 14: 30

Problem 15: 63.3

Problem 16: 18

Problem 17: 5184

Problem 18: 13.3

Problem 19: 1323

Problem 20: 6

ZIML June 2019 Division M

Problem 1:	6	Problem 11:	12
Problem 2:	20	Problem 12:	5
Problem 3:	8	Problem 13:	105
Problem 4:	1200	Problem 14:	46656
Problem 5:	29	Problem 15:	100
Problem 6:	20	Problem 16:	42
Problem 7:	9725	Problem 17:	10
Problem 8:	692	Problem 18:	3360
Problem 9:	135	Problem 19:	6
Problem 10:	2880	Problem 20:	8

www.ingramcontent.com/pod-product-compliance
Lightning Source LLC
Chambersburg PA
CBHW071202160426
43196CB00011B/2167